THE BRIDGE

From Old to New in Christian Belief

THE BRIDGE

From Old to New in Christian Belief

SEEF KONIJN

ABBEY PRESS
ST. MEINRAD, INDIANA 47577
1973

First published as *Ter Overbrugging*, © 1971 Gooi & Sticht NV, Hilversum
Translated into English by Hubert Hoskins
© English translation 1973 Geoffrey Chapman Publishers,
a division of Crowell Collier Macmillan Publishers Ltd

ISBN 0 225 65975 1
First published this edition, 1973
Library of Congress Catalogue Card Number: 73—86288

Contents

Preface

This little book is the result of three years of probing, talking, discussion and study. It has grown out of my work in talking to adults about religion. It is not intended to be a round-up of all the new thinking going on in matters of religion and belief. I have worked with a number of groups in the last few years, and the question that keeps on cropping up time and time again is: how do the beliefs we were brought up in connect with what is being taught today? how has the new grown out of the old?

That is why I have called this book *The Bridge: from old to new in Christian belief.* My intention has been to write a simple book that can be read without too much effort, and I have written it particularly for people who feel ill at ease in the present religious atmosphere, because they have grown out of the way they were brought up but don't feel at home with modern attitudes either.

The subjects I deal with are limited; I have not attempted to cover every question of doctrine or practice. My aim has been to use certain fundamental facts about the religious scene to show how there is a connecting thread running through the whole renewal movement. So don't expect this book to provide answers: it offers no answers, but rather a direction along which we have to go forward, in faith.

My hope is that many people will find this book useful, and that it will give them a foothold in the present and faith in the future. Discussion groups should be able to make use of it, and I hope, too, that many of the clergy who have the job of instructing adults will turn to it from time to time.

SEEF KONIJN

1 Getting our bearings

Most of us were brought up in a more or less tranquil climate. There was a recognizable order of things. You knew where you stood and what you must conform to, whether in the social or the religious sphere.

There were changes going on, of course; but compared with the rapids sweeping us along today, life was very much like an unruffled sheet of water. Typical of this was the atmosphere of the old catechisms. Starting with the question: 'Who made you? Why did God make you?' our whole faith was set out in the clearest possible terms. To every question there was a plain answer. And the answers parents had learnt were learnt in turn by their offspring—yet today these answers seem less and less comprehensible.

A great deal has happened in recent years. What was going on all the time beneath the surface has now emerged into the clear light of day. I do not exaggerate when I say that we are living now in a totally different world; that we are quite different human beings in the making, as it were. And that, of course, has immediate consequences for the way we live out our beliefs and the way we express them in words.

One might perhaps summarize the process of development we are undergoing in a religious context like this: what we are experiencing just now is a development *from belief to believing, from 'faith' to 'having faith'*. I mean by *'belief'* accepting a body of religious truths which one cannot see any good reason for, but which one accepts on someone else's authority. Here faith and church affiliation are closely related. This kind of belief you can lose, you can abandon, you can put it aside, just as you might a pile of books, and people do talk like this about 'losing the faith' and so on. *Believing* has much more to do with an attitude than with acceptance of this or that 'truth'. You can see, for instance, that the imparting of knowledge has a far smaller place in the teaching of religion than it used to do. Believing, having faith, is much more a question of a believing attitude, striking a note of release and trust, in which truthfulness rates higher perhaps than 'truth'. I should say rather : than formulations of the truth. More and more we are coming to realize that is it not possible to encapsulate the truth in a form of words. So it is not wisdom to wave dogmas around or be ready to swear by them. If a truth *is* expressed in that way, we must regard it as a signpost, some-thing to assist the people of a particular period, an attempt to put into words, as well as one can, and for that period of time, the real substance of what we believe. In our own day we are giving verbal expression to new aspects of that same mystery of faith; yet not even we can utter the final word. If we realize this, we are bound to adopt a less arbitrary, more relative attitude to things : and this is a good thing.

Such an approach will make a person more generous, more liberal in outlook, without in any way compromising his deepest convictions. There is no longer any need for us to be at one another's throats over this, that or the other truth—although this does, alas, still happen. *A New Catechism*, first published in Holland and now known throughout the world as 'the Dutch catechism', has this to say about why expressions of faith change:

> 'Councils of the church did not aim at determining exhaus-tively and for all time all the truth of the mystery. The words they used were often formulations meant to defend very definite Christian truths and values at a certain period, against certain errors. To understand properly the teachings of the councils, one must always ask what Christian and evangelical values were at stake at the time? When we know what was being defended, we must then proclaim the same truths in the language of our own day' (p. 334).

The shift taking place at the moment might also be character-ized by saying that we are moving from a situation where we are *obedient church members* more and more toward being *mature, 'enfranchized' Christians*. This is bound up with, for instance, the different way we feel about authority and react to it. You can see signs of this in almost every area of life. For the believer it means that his priest or minister no longer settles everything for him, no longer decides for him in matters of conscience. It is more a case of his being inspired by them to find out for himself what his responsibility is as a Christian, in church and society. Finally, we might describe what is going on by saying that we are on the move from the old catechism to the new. By this I mean that the whole atmosphere is changing. The old question-and-answer game was fairly cut and dried; you didn't ask sup-plementaries. But the idea that everything is self-evident has gone for good.

What parents once learnt and what their children are being taught today are two quite different things; so that anyone who does not want to be left stranded is obliged to take new bearings amid the host of questions crowding in upon him. Those ques-tions can no longer be thought out of existence or out of our lives. That may not be a very nice feeling; but on the other hand it does give the man or woman of our time a chance to remain alive and flexible and full of activity to the very end. It is an attitude to life that suits well with the technical climate we are living in. The philosopher, Wittgenstein, summed up this frame of mind when he stated that whatever is said should be said clearly; if it cannot be said clearly, it should not be said at all. That is an attitude conditioned by science and technology. It is a hard-headed, enquiring attitude that you find in a growing number of people today, and especially in the young. They are less and less ready to accept 'the done thing'. More and more they insist on asking : what's the *point* of it, *what's in it for me*? They are not very readily impressed by the 'experience of life' which older people like to appeal to; nor are they willing to be led up the garden by high-sounding phrases. They want to do their own prospecting and discover for themselves what life is about—and religion, too. They are no longer prepared to be packed off to church simply because that is what people do, or ought to do. There are risks attached to such an attitude—but opportunities as well, and in particular the opportunity to live one's life with a quality of frankness and freshness and authenti-city, and to expose at once any sort of sham or lack of honesty and truthfulness.

You may say : I can't keep up; the times have stolen a march on me. And, of course, you can react very negatively to everything that is of today. Yet is that a very scriptural approach? Can you put your trust in that attitude? Are you thereby helping to build a better future? We are on the move. From the Faith to having faith. From the stage of being ecclesiastical minors, under-age church members, to being responsible, enfranchized Christians. From the climate of the old catechism to that of the new. Can we see the good in this onward movement? Dare we set the pace? It is true, isn't it, that anybody who tries to stop now is likely to seize up altogether?

2 'I believe in God, the Father Almighty'

Does this phrase express anything real in experience?

At the start of this book I want to take a steady look at our experience of God, of the presence of God in our lives; for it is precisely over this central core of our religious awareness and the way we speak about it that the greatest confusion prevails. People feel more and more uneasy with what they used to be taught about God. When you utter the name of God, what is it you are really saying? What are you talking about? Questions like this are becoming more common. One of the people here in Holland who has urged us to be very cautious in speaking about God is Cornelis Verhoeven. In his book *Rondom de Leegte* he says :

> 'I concede no authority whatever in this matter to myself any more than to theologians and philosophers. Any claim to special knowledge about God is absurd and possibly blasphemous. At the very most one can be expert in the history of the conceptual representation of a god, in so far as that has been placed on record. . . . Although there is undoubtedly nothing more important than religion, I always find it extraordinarily ludicrous when a number of people meet to chatter and natter and discuss and swop ideas about God. To chatter about God in the surroundings of a rather cosy get-together over coffee and cigars is not on. One cannot talk about God in such circumstances—at any rate, not about God as a reality. If God is a reality, there is nothing to discuss' (p. 155).

The question we must ask ourselves is this : where does it come from, this name of God, Yahweh, the Lord, Father, in the Bible?

13

The Bridge

In what circumstances was it originally used? We were always taught that God revealed himself to men. He made his name known to us. That is true. Yet we must not take this to mean that God simply, all at once, and in person, appeared to man and whispered his name in his ear. Biblical criticism has let us get beyond that. The stories about God and his name in the Bible are figurative or dramatic stories about overwhelming human experiences. Then what human experiences do we encounter in the biblical happening where the name of Yahweh, the Lord, or the name Father is used.

Experiences of God in the Bible

Let's take a closer look at a few stories in the Bible. I want to begin with *Jacob*, one of the ancestors of the Jewish people. You all know about him. In the meanest possible way he filched his brother Esau's birthright. First by giving him that mess of potage; and then by his villainous behaviour in getting his blind father Isaac's blessing before his brother could get it. This made Esau furious. The only thing for Jacob to do then was to get out of the way. Far away from his own country he took refuge with an uncle and worked for him as a shepherd for twenty years. He acquired a large flock and became a wealthy man. But this brought Jacob no happiness at all. He longed to get back to the place where he really belonged, to the man who was his nearest kin, his brother, Esau. The thought was always in his mind; and the day came when he set off with all his possessions. Yet all the time he was scared. And the evening before he was to meet his brother he was beside himself, he could not stand it any more. His heart sank into his boots. That night he wanted to be completely alone. Everything looked totally black. He was in the throes of a major crisis. Then comes the splendid story of Jacob's nocturnal wrestling with a man (Genesis 32:23–32). You simply must read it. It is a 'captured' experience of God. Who is this man he fought with? Was it his brother Esau? Was it his own conscience? Was it God? Jacob won the fight. As the struggle ended, it grew light. He was through the main crisis. He felt reborn. Now he was equal to the trials that awaited him. He had recovered his confidence; and he felt lifted above himself. This event made such an impression on Jacob that he bore the mark of it for the rest

14

of his life. The writer says that as a result of the fight Jacob's hip was permanently dislocated. He had experienced something like a presence—an encircling, heartening presence. From that moment he was called not Jacob but Israel: which means, wrestling with God. His name has also come to be the name of the whole Jewish people. And we Christians still call ourselves the *new* Israel. A wrestling with God. The name is a mandate, the task of a lifetime, from which there can be no final release.

We see the same kind of thing happening in the life of *Moses*. To save his life Moses fled from Egypt. He became a shepherd. But the fact that he was leading a quiet life while many of his kinsfolk were in such desperate straits made him uncomfortable. It wouldn't leave him alone. With his Egyptian upbringing, wasn't he the obvious man to get things moving, to try and liberate his people? But every time the idea came into his head he couldn't face it. He went through a period of great trouble. There is always a long gap between seeing what one's duty is and actually doing it. However, in the end the gap was closed. Moses went to the Pharaoh. But, in his eyes, to have reached that point was no credit to him. This whole process of growth is cast in the form of a dialogue between Yahweh and Moses, against the background of the burning bush (Exodus 3 and 4).

Moses came up with one objection after another; but Yahweh overcame them all—five times, in fact. And in the middle of the dialogue was heard this name: Yahweh. It means: I shall be (there), I will not let go of you. The name expresses exactly what Moses experienced: the whole atmosphere of confidence in a successful outcome, by which he felt surrounded, this heartening presence enabling him to make the venture. He was lifted above himself. The same thing happened after the scene with the golden calf. Moses was so disillusioned with his people that he wanted to throw in his hand. If that was the way they were, he was finished with them. He was completely defeated. But once again he came through the crisis. This event, too, is told in a moving narrative in which Moses felt a supporting presence close by him, helping him through the crisis.

The story ends like this: 'And Yahweh said: "Here is a place beside me. You must stand on the rock, and when my glory passes by, I will put you in a cleft of the rock and shield you with my hand while I pass by. Then I will take my hand away and you shall see the back of me; but my face is not to be seen".'

Only afterwards is Moses able to say: that must have been Yahweh. An almost childish story.

Behind this kind of tale lie kindred experiences. Quite common experiences of a sort we too are familiar with. Jacob dare not take another step for fear of his brother. Moses is without the strength to do what he believes he should do. And then eventually each reaches the point where 'it's not up to me any more'. Familiar situations. But in them those men came up against values in their lives of a sort that you can acquire but cannot get by force. You can't force yourself to have faith in the future. It is precisely at such moments that the name of Yahweh occurs. At such moments we find Jesus at prayer, and the name 'Father' is uttered. When his end seems inevitable, Jesus retires with a few disciples on to the mountain. The confidence-imparting presence becomes visible, as it were, in the glory of transfiguration. Strengthened and made resolute, Jesus comes down from the mountain. Again, in the Garden of Olives, he seems to pray himself through the crisis. He feels such complete trust in this intimate presence that instead of 'Yahweh' he uses the child's word for father, 'abba': 'daddy'.

These are ordinary situations and ordinary human experiences. Each of us has them from time to time. We can recognize ourselves in Jacob, in Moses, in Jesus.

But the question is: in that kind of situation do we too have such a powerful experience of that surrounding presence that the name 'Yahweh' or 'Father' springs to our lips? Or do we just say: absolutely terrific—if only one could believe it! Do we have experiences in our life that we could describe as divine? These are important questions for us and for our religious life; for I believe that the crisis in religion, in our experience of faith, stems very largely from the fact that faith and life have drifted too far apart; that for many people it has ceased to be obvious that religious belief has anything to do with the life of every day. That is why believing in God has become simply superfluous for a lot of people. After all, they say, things still go on without God. What I want to do is make a whole once more of faith and life. But I shall come back to that later on.

16

Man in search of himself

Every single human being is on the move toward himself, toward his full development. He has the potential for continuous growth, for reaching an ever greater measure of maturity. He can grow by means of contacts, experiences, the moments of joy and sorrow that life affords him. He can become suddenly aware at times that a lot of things happen in his life on which he has no grip at all and which he is unable to control. What really makes life worth living, worth troubling about, is not there for the taking. With all his money, his technology, his power, man is helpless in this respect. He can only come with open hand, ready to receive.

That is the most he can be—the one who receives. Just think of the experiences of Jacob and Moses that I have been telling you about. These things simply descend upon a man; they come over him. But what is it, you may ask, that the individual experiences at moments of this sort? It always entails an emotional activity, I think, the act of believing, trusting, cherishing. When a person feels these emotions invading his life, he experiences transport, delight and happiness. But then at the same time he realizes just how dependent he is. There is much that man can do; and he is going to be able to do more and more in the future. He may perhaps succeed in increasing his life-span by fifty years. But in his most inward self, touched by the dictates of chance and fortune, he makes the discovery that his life is not under his own control. After all, you can't force yourself to have faith in the future. You can't buy love. That is why we have always referred to having faith, hoping and loving as divine virtues, as pearls in our lives which may fall into our lap but which are not ours to command. I believe it is precisely these virtues, these values of faith, hope and love that Jesus is on about when he speaks in the gospel about the kingdom of God. They are such disconcerting realities that it is hard for us to talk about them. Clutch at them, and they invariably slip your grasp; which is why Jesus nearly always speaks in imaginary parables when he wants to express the mysteries of God's kingdom by the use of words. Only think of the sower, the mustard-seed, the pearl of great price. And what images have not been found in our search to express in words the feelings of love between man and woman. How rich in pictorial images are the stories centred around Jacob and Moses—and the account of Jesus' glorification on the mountain!

I would sum it all up like this: every individual wants to achieve happiness. Some look for it too much on the surface of life. They want to make money or technological achievement or power the guarantee of their happiness. But they do not really succeed. Others, penetrating much deeper, manage to attain real happiness. Think of Jacob, Moses, Francis of Assissi and many more. We Christians believe that Jesus thrust through to the ultimate depths. He explored and experienced the potentialities of human existence more profoundly than anyone else. He disclosed, revealed, what (or who) man can really be; and in doing that he gave human life a richer, more coherent perspective than ever before. Like no other person he was on his own, he was self-contained. But as we have seen, the happier a person is, the more he realizes that this happiness is a gift. That is why Jesus was more powerfully aware than we are of how dependent he was. Both his experience of happiness and his experience of dependence one expressed in that one word, that one name, Father.

Although life is too rich, of course, to be netted and pinned down in a diagram, this may perhaps help to make some things clearer.

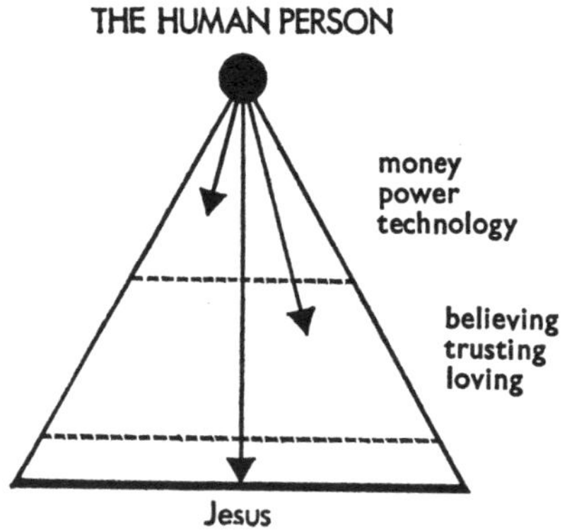

We can represent the possibilities in man's life by means of a triangle. Narrow at the top, as man penetrates deeper the happiness, the perspective, becomes broader and more copious. However, man is inclined to keep a tight hold on his luck and to stay inside the top sector. But to reach happiness he must be able to thrust right through money, technology and power. Then true religion may be awakened.

What should our attitude be?

We are now in a position to ask why it is that one person has these experiences and another not, why one person is of the believing sort and another not. I have shown that Jacob and Moses were confronted with very common situations such as we all encounter from time to time. Only many of us live through this kind of situation without being greatly affected; and many of us come through such a crisis. But that doesn't astonish us. We take it all as a matter of course and go on our way without so much as a surprised glance around us.

The fact is, most of us take our lives more or less for granted. There are only a few people for whom the ordinary is quite marvellous. What such people evince is a particular kind of life. With true openness of mind they let things invade them, come at them. They are receptive to what is going on. Most of us are stopped short only by sensational news. The first man steps on to the moon. Then a thrill really does go through you. But the second time round it is already beginning to be stale news; and so we live, from one sensation to another. Yet I believe it to be a greater miracle that a couple can love each other for a lifetime than that two people land on the moon.

So, too, for the Jews the journey from Egypt through the wilderness was an ordinary sort of event, in the long term even a very tedious one. They made that quite obvious. But Moses saw more deeply. He saw more. He saw what was really happening. And on his perspective, his way of seeing things, a whole people was nourished and was able to live. When he was around, everything could be its real self. To be able to believe and hope and love one needs a childlike attitude to things. The child has a keen eye, knows how to stand amazed. Things *mean* more to a child than to us grown-ups; but it soon grows to be like us. A grown-up wants to use things, to have them at his beck and call. Only occasionally does this childlike receptiveness come to the surface in us again. At the start of spring; on a fine winter's evening; on our holidays. Then we are arrested by buildings and by vistas which normally we would not even see. Or when a husband and wife have a baby. Notice the word 'have'. You can tell just how insensitive people are who talk about 'making' a baby. But these things are over in a flash. And it may well happen that even on holiday people look without actually seeing, that they take things so completely for granted that they crush them out of existence. The posture is one of unbelief. It is the child in us that Jesus tries so hard to keep alive. All his sayings about what is essentially childlike within us have to do with the kingdom of God.

'Unless a man is born again, he cannot see the kingdom of God' (John 3:3). 'Anyone who does not accept the kingdom of God like a child will not be able to enter it' (Mark 10:15). Other sayings, too, are to be interpreted in this vein: 'It is easier for a camel to go through the eye of a needle than for a rich man to enter the kingdom of God' (Matthew 19:24). I would hope that in this way being a believing person will gradually come to have a different meaning for you.

Can such experiences be handed on?

I have said that experiencing God, being aware of God, springs out of ordinary human experiences. Experiences which we all have: getting through a crisis, resolving a deadlock, picking up the pieces and carrying on. They are experiences with always a recurrent element of faith, of trust, of love in them. It just leaps up at you. Money, technology, power, these can do nothing to help, will get you nowhere. In situations of this kind people feel that they have somehow crossed a barrier and they begin at last to speak about God.

I have told of Jacob and Moses. Those were very personal experiences of happiness, of the gift of courage. Yet at the same time there is a sense of dependence, a realization that what is most valuable in one's life is simply given to one.

People who are open to such experiences are very much taken up with them and find it has become impossible to rationalize the experiences out of existence. They were never happier than at such moments. Jacob is one who carried the marks of what had happened to him for the rest of his life. The story records that after the struggle he was permanently lame. Obviously, such people want others to share this happiness of theirs; and when men like Jacob and Moses tell of their experiences, others are fired by them and say: 'If that is the outcome, this Yahweh must be at the centre of our lives as well; he must be our God, too!' Then the original experience gets clothed in words—and first in a name: Yahweh, Father. Then in a creed: I believe in God, the almighty Father. Later still, in a doctrine, a theory. The danger then is that others will carry this name into their lives, but without any overtones of that wealth of experience belonging to those who, however falteringly, had first uttered it.

To convey an experience of the divine to another person is hard enough. It is harder still to pass it on to the next generation. It can happen that uttering the name 'Yahweh' ceases to be the expression of a personal experience and becomes just an imitation of other people. Then it is something that comes from outside, something that you simply pick up. The first generation is tremendously enriched through these experiences. For the second generation there is no longer any real discovery. The danger is that in taking it over they will take it all for granted. Religion can then easily become something that comes at us from outside and has little to do with our own mode of living. Religion and life then become two worlds that barely affect each other.

The Bible contains some fierce protests against this divergence between religion and life. 'What are your endless sacrifices to me? . . . Search for justice, help the oppressed, be just to the orphan, plead for the widow' (Isaiah 1:10, 17). Jesus, too, fought against this separation: 'It is not those who say to me "Lord, Lord" who will enter the kingdom of heaven, but the person who does the will of my Father in heaven' (Matthew 7:21).

A substantial part of all the problems confronting us in the area of religion nowadays consists in precisely this divorce between heaven and earth, between church and world, between what we believe and how we live. I have already touched on that.

For many people religion is not a living expression, not an articulation of their deepest feelings any more. So belief becomes unimportant, irrelevant. They can get by without it, in any case, and so they do. When we hear Jacob, Moses or Jesus talk about the bond linking them with Yahweh, they don't mean some kind of take-it-or-leave-it relationship. When they say 'I believe in

Yahweh', what they mean is : I believe that life has a profound significance, I believe in myself. For them believing cannot be separated from living. Anyone who has experienced living as believing knows what it can mean to be a human being.

For a lot of people nowadays being religious does not give a genuine dimension of depth to their lives; it is more an alienating factor, encroaching on their lives from outside. So many formulations are out of date and therefore no longer provide the words to describe our experience of life as we live it today; so there is a considerable risk that many people will no longer associate really profound experiences with their religion. Thus there are parents who cannot see that infant baptism adds another and deeper dimension to their own situation. They regard baptism as an alien element that is irrelevant to their real life. And there are people who cannot relate a period of depression in their lives to the fact of being a believer : 'faith has to do with quite other things'.

Perhaps it will make things clearer if I finish off the diagram.

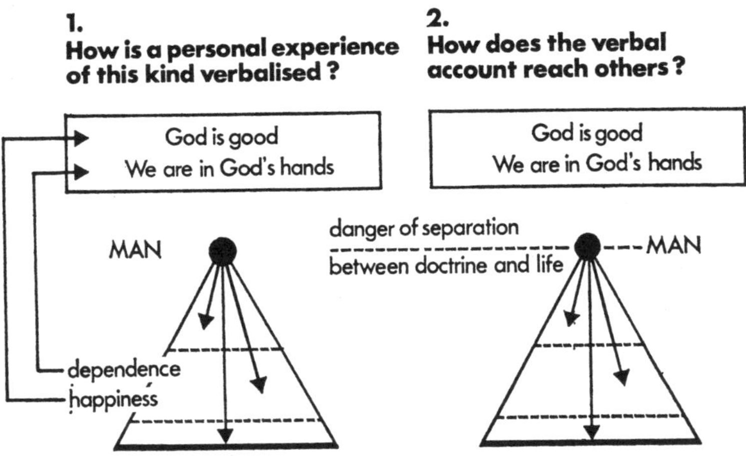

It is very difficult to convey experiences that are quite personal. How can you communicate the whole world of feeling? In being communicated to other people, personal experiences quickly become generalized. When a man like Moses, for instance, passes on his tremendous experience of happiness to his people, it comes out as 'Yahweh is good'. When he puts across his strong sense of dependence, it sounds something like this: 'Yahweh is creator; we are in his hands'. That is a profession of belief. That is a doctrine. The danger, as always, is that those who hear these words will not be able to complete the connection between the doctrine—the theory—and their own lives.

In the same way the replies provided by the old catechism came upon us from on high. We learned them, but as often as not failed to make them our own. For let us be honest: the answers we used to learn were answers to questions that were not *our* questions. 'Why did God make you?' is a question we have never really wrestled with. We simply learnt the right answer. But nowadays we want to know the value of the answers before we will learn them. And in this turbulent and baffling age it is usually with a sigh that we voice the question: what is the real point of life? That *does* come from our depths. It is a question that keeps cropping up—and one that we shall never finally resolve. Whatever answers may be given, they are all approximations conditioned by time and circumstance. Our own answer must be tested, as it were, by the touchstone of those who have wrestled with this question in times past, especially in the Bible, but also of those who wrestle with it here and now in our own time, when so many people are troubled about the meaning of their lives. Obviously, there is no clear, simple answer.

If the name of God does crop up in our lives, it can only do so at the point where a man plumbs the depths of his existence in relation with others; where in total trust he feels himself caught up into a larger whole; where following in the steps of others he becomes aware of a prospect in his life, an unbounded prospect.

This way of thinking has its consequences

If God does become a conscious issue in our lives, that has many consequences. It means, for instance, that religious education is less and less a matter of putting across an elaborate body of teaching, more and more a question of inducing a proper attitude to life. The chief thing must be learning how to penetrate into the depths of our existence and how to articulate that experience. For this we need to live in a spirit of receptiveness and wonderment. Then religion and life will no longer be two disparate realities; and a false idea of God can be avoided. We always run the risk of basing ourselves on a more or less circumscribed view of God : God is good; God cares; God wants me to do this or that. The result is that we start out from generalizations. Actually, we can only start from our own experience as human beings. That was in point of fact the sole starting-point in the Bible. Today we see more compellingly than ever that it must still be the only starting-point.

This entails an adjustment in our way of detecting whether somebody is or is not a 'man of faith'. The point is not in the first instance whether a person embraces some *doctrine* or other, but whether his life-style is the right one. The doctrine, the theory as such, is always bound to be the verbalized expression of this attitude to life. Attempts at renewal are often countered nowadays with the weapon of the church's official teaching. In this searching, probing period it is understandable that a lot of people should try to cling hard to the official teaching of the church. But life is no longer covered by that teaching. Every age has its way of contending with God and on his account. It is a struggle we must not be afraid to approve. Religion is never something clearly defined and written down. Of course, a certain direction may be presented to us from time to time; but in a time like ours, a time of rapid change, that may easily give rise to false expectations. Having faith is not a matter of accepting this or that particular doctrine so much as of being ready at all times to undertake the struggle in our own lives. Having faith means starting out again and again as Jacob, in order to become Israel. Then the prospect may lighten.

3 'Secularization'

Secularization! A word that has been on almost everyone's lips in recent years—so you must surely have come across it. It is a sort of handle for getting a grip on present-day trends in religion and on the whole religious scene.

But what does the word really mean? 'Secularization' comes from the Latin *saeculum*, world. You might define secularization, therefore, as 'the world's coming to be the world'. It is a strange way of talking, really. It implies that previously the world was not genuinely world at all. The world was not itself, could not be itself. It was confused, mixed up with gods, with God. Secularization denotes the process whereby the world and God get room to be themselves.

A man in the Cameroon had built himself a house. He did not go and live in it. He daren't. For the moment he went inside he would die—or so he thought; because the house was built in the wrong place and certain rituals had not been duly observed. A house in these circumstances is not yet a house; and any real freedom for man is not yet a possibility. There is fear and there is menace. Nature is infected by supernature. We have all heard tell of the sacred cows in certain parts of India. No person is allowed to touch them, not even a vet. A man is not permitted to do what would be of advantage to himself and to the animal. Missionaries could, I think, tell a whole lot of similar tales. Our own remote ancestors lived like this, in fear and trembling. Behind thunder and lightning, rain and drought, sickness and health, lurked for them all sorts of gods and goddesses. Elusive, unaccountable, jealous beings. You couldn't rely on them. All you could do was offer sacrifices and so keep them as much as possible in a friendly mood. A perpetual menace.

When we believe, as the Bible makes it possible for us to do, we are delivered from that menace. I must try and elucidate this business of believing for you in more detail. In the perspective provided by such belief everything can come to be itself, can be itself. In that perspective a disease is a disease, a thunderstorm is a thunderstorm. We need no longer go in fear of every conceivable sort of evil spirit as the agents responsible for storm and disease. That is a tremendous liberation—and a large part of secularization too. Man, the world, can be wholly themselves. And yet in Christianity, as it has worked out in practice, there has been a recurrent mix-up between the world and God, between man and God. This has meant that neither God nor man could 'be themselves'—they have got in each other's way, so to speak. As a result, our whole concept of the divine enshrined a definite element of competition between God and man. We are always in danger of drawing a sharp contrast, with God on one side and man's technical achievement on the other. Where you have technology, there is no further room for God. The result is that in easy stages we assert that God is dead. Let us listen for a moment to what the Dutch catechism has to say about this.

> 'In earlier times men were inclined to see God at work precisely where the natural causes of things were unknown. It was taken for granted that he was at work in all that existed, but very often he was supposed to be most intimately present where strange and inexplicable things happened, such as the sudden onset or cessation of a tempest or an epidemic. His presence was felt in particular outside the ordinary course of events. Thus he was seen perhaps more readily in the blessing over the sick than in the skill of the doctor. . . . The more a creature is itself, the more God is active in it. God's action does not consist of his pushing aside what he has created, but of his bringing it to be itself as fully as possible, and man most of all' (*New Catechism*, p. 491).

During the period when science and technology were still in their infancy a whole lot of things defied explanation. It was not known where they came from, how they were to be accounted for, how one should react to them. And where man felt himself at a loss, God was slotted in. Throughout that period this was, of course, a frequent occurrence. But as science and technology advance, so do we acquire a better and better understanding of the laws governing man and the world. That *may* mean that there is less need for God to be brought into it. But it is getting increasingly hard for us to speak about God as the One who supplies the deficiencies in our human knowledge, who fills in the gaps where we are unable to do so. God is not located at the outer edge of our life. He is right in the middle of it. The god who is obliged to retreat on all fronts in the face of our technological discoveries is a god we ourselves have projected. Yet it is certainly an image that has deep roots within us. Man has no need to pray for this or that, if he can cope perfectly well by himself. Similarly, some people, when they pray 'Give us this day our daily bread' think: how crazy can you get; I've earned my bread by my own efforts. As though God and man were mutually exclusive.

Anyone who thinks on those lines is making a god 'after his own image'; and when that happens, God cannot be himself. Nor, for that matter, can man. And such a person will argue that as technology forges ahead, so there will be less and less that comes under the aegis of God. Eventually, a time will come when God will have vanished from the world altogether.

Let me try and illustrate that with another diagram.

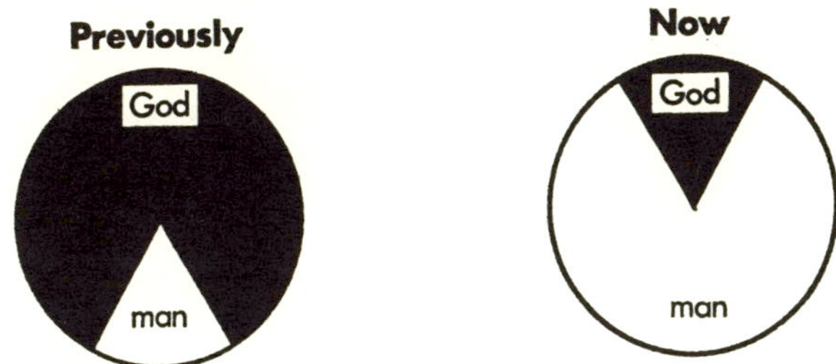

The circle stands for the whole area of man's life, its scope and outreach. At one time, most of this was unknown territory. It was a case of 'God behind me, God before me'. But now man has very largely taken control of his existence. The total disappearance of God from our world is imminent.

A few years ago, during a TV 'teach-in' on the Death of God, someone said: 'Every car that comes along means a step back for God, another spade of sand tossed on to God's grave.'

Even among believers this notion of God persists. At about the same time a minister said to his congregation : 'Anybody who has his children inoculated against polio has no trust in God. If you trust in God you must also trust your children won't fall ill.' As though God and human expertise were mutually incompatible! God works *through* man. What man has to do is what God gives him to do.

So there has been a sort of confusion, a mix-up, as it were, between the world and God. For instance, documents produced by the church during the last century persistently connected poverty with God's plans and purposes for man. Marx saw poverty as an economic problem. The church's documents were simply confusing God with the social phenomenon of poverty.

Even quite recently a natural phenomenon was attributed to God. During an earthquake in Sicily, the bishop appeared on television and said 'God is shaking us up'. He was muddling God with the forces of nature. Such confusion is highly dangerous; for where God and the world are confused with each other there can be no place for science and technology. If you are persuaded that a disease is caused by a divine being, there is not much sense in starting to look for a satisfactory cure. You will turn to a priest or a magician, not to a doctor. If you are really convinced that storms are brought about by a supernatural being, there is not much sense in trying to find some effective counter-measure. You will, of course, offer sacrifices. Result : no lightning-conductor. And the further danger is that if technology does nevertheless make progress, it will usually do so from a mental attitude wholly divorced from religion. *In principle*, biblical faith has paved the way for technology; so it is not surprising that technology has sprung up and flourished mightily in those parts of the world most influenced by Christianity.

In practice, however, the same confusion between God and the world has occurred in Christianity, too. I have been into that already. Understandably, therefore, the church has greeted scientific discoveries and technological inventions with a certain amount of suspicion. One has only to recall the trial of Galileo in 1616. Not all church dignitaries, alas, have agreed with Cardinal Baronius, who in Copernicus' day observed that the scriptures were written to instruct us 'not how heaven works but only how to get there'. Scientific enquiry seemed to threaten the religious view of man and the world. The argument apparently went like this: God's creation is good; so anybody who wants to change anything in it is possessed by the devil. Thus man was prevented from discovering his own potential and his proper mission. He was not yet free, not yet secularized. So we see that for a long time wisdom and science brought no improvement in man's lot.

Yet despite the reserved attitude of the church, technology has moved forward. The church's task is to lead man to God. If God and the world are indistinguishable, then the church is going to try and take the whole life of society under its charge. As we all know, there has been plenty of that kind of thing. Not long ago, almost everything, from setting up a family to dancing and playing football, was organized and run by the church. That is why secularization is not only the process whereby God and the world are distinguished and separated—a process in which man attains his majority, as it were, and assumes responsibility for the whole turn of events, for his own affairs; it also means that all the various departments and areas of man's life are withdrawn from the church's control. It entails throwing off a yoke that hindered and even prevented their proper, autonomous development. It is a process of self-discovery. That is also why the process of secularization has gone hand in hand with a continuing conflict with the churches.

Until recently, therefore, secularization has been viewed by believers with disfavour. Many still reject it; but a growing number are ready to evaluate it in positive terms. After all, what is at issue is the world's liberation into responsibility before God. Of course, secularization may reach a point where not only the gods but any religious consciousness whatever is left out of account. But that there is absolutely no necessity for that to happen I hope to make clear to you in what follows.

4 Can we go on praying in the same old way?

If a man speaks *about* God in a different way, when he comes to speak *with* God that will be different, too. So against the background of what has already been said I want now to go further into the question of prayer. Prayer could be described as the living, beating heart of every religion. It is also the thermometer that tells us what sort of condition religion and religious experience are in. Most of us do less praying than used to be the case. The naturalness, the spontaneity, with which we once said our prayers has to a great extent evaporated. What are we to make of that? Some of us feel that this inability to pray as we used to means that our faith has suffered a defeat. Others are glad that in our prayers we do not stick so firmly to set formulas. Others again find that their work and their praying are one and the same thing. Yes, indeed; we are far from having sorted out this question. What does praying mean to us? And what forms can our praying take? Here, there and everywhere, we notice misgivings about praying the way people have done for so many years.

What do we really want of God?

You will recall that services of intercession were held in the United States for the unlucky Apollo XIII astronauts; and you may also remember that not everybody gave those services a kind reception. They prompted various reactions and comments, of which I propose to mention only three. These should give us an idea of what is really at issue when we talk about praying. 'The astronauts got back safely thanks to modern technology and the

30

air-control centre at Houston. It had nothing to do with prayer' was the reaction of one commentator on the radio. 'They organize pray-ins for the astronauts; but America has so far never organized pray-ins for her soldiers fighting in Vietnam, let alone for the Vietnamese whom those soldiers have been bombarding.' And I read in a certain newspaper: 'Are the defoliants and poison gasses used in Vietnam preordained by the same God who brought Lovell and his men safely back to earth?' The writer adds, somewhat cynically: 'I am not yet all that much of a believer; so I am more inclined than some may be to leave God out of it. After all, even without God the going is hard enough.'

This last remark reminds me of the moving story about Beau Jack, an illiterate shoe-shine boy who became a professional boxer and lightweight champion of the world. Someone once said to him: 'I've heard it said that you pray before every match.' 'That's right,' said Jack, with a broad grin, 'I pray that nobody will get hurt. And then I pray that it will be a good fight.' 'But don't you ever pray that you'll win?' 'No,' he said. 'Supposing I did. And the other chap prays that he will win too. And then what is God to do?'

Yes, well. What is God to do then? British and Germans prayed simultaneously for victory. Americans pray, North Vietnamese pray, South Vietnamese pray. What is God to do? Should God do anything?

The prayer uttered when the astronauts had arrived safe and sound aboard ship may perhaps have moved you: 'Through your mercy and through their skill the astronauts have returned to earth.' That sounds very different from what the radio commentator had said: 'Not by prayer but thanks to modern technology.'

We are always in danger of falling into the same error—the error of setting up a sharp opposition between God and technology, like this: where we have technology there is no room for God; and so prayer becomes superfluous. It means in fact that God is pronounced 'dead'. I have already tried to pinpoint this particular danger. When God and man are seen as in competition, false ways of making use of prayer will be lying in wait to entrap us. Prayer will be regarded as one means among many others: if one should prove helpful, then there's no need to try any of the others. There is the further danger that we shall resort to prayer without having tried to find out what we can do for ourselves, at the human level. Prayer can then become a flight from reality, a means of escape. A prayer which we may consider to be real and genuine enough may be an alibi, therefore, an excuse for not having to do anything. Somebody was once asked: 'What did you do for the Jews in the war?' He said: 'I didn't actually shelter anyone; but I did pray for them a great deal.' I don't think one could be very proud of a reply like that. It is playing safe yourself whilst praying for others, sending so many words on up to a higher being, instead of offering a hand to the human beings at your side.

Prayer as the verbal expression of our mission in life

In our best moments we become aware of our life as a present, a gift. For instance, at those times when every prospect pleases or we are intensely happy with someone. Yet we know only too well that our life is also a mission and a task; or perhaps we might do better to say that our life is a giving of ourselves, a kind of surrender. For we are more than ever convinced that our life can only become fully human when our attitude is one of service. But what form that service should take can never be settled in advance. It requires of us an attitude of attentive concern.

You might say: God issues his call to us within the situation in which we find ourselves. God approaches us through that whole network of human relationships in which we are involved. It is there that our life's mission is drafted, so to speak, from one day to another. I said that we are sometimes aware of our life as a gift. When that happens, the appropriate thing is to render thanks. But more often life presents itself to us as a task calling for dedication; and in that situation the proper thing is supplication. This is what we usually have in mind when we talk about praying. Doesn't that say a lot about the way we live?

In prayer we try to listen out for, and to hear, God's voice—as that voice finds expression within the totality of our living. In prayer we try in all honesty to get a clear idea what is being asked of us. That is something of the utmost importance; for whether we fulfil the task laid upon us will decide whether or not we are living life to the full, whether or not we are living it whole, whether or not wellbeing and happiness are ours.

I have linked prayer of petition, 'asking' prayer, to the business of getting on with the task awaiting us. You see now, I hope, the danger inherent in the saying: to pray is to work. This is something one often hears said. And of course there is something in it. You can, after all, regard your whole life as a journeying to God, a journey toward your true self. In that sense the whole of life might be described as a prayer—prayer in a very broad sense indeed, though. As you live your life you learn to recognize your own peculiar task and you fulfil it in the way you actually live. At least, that is feasible. But we come to call it prayer only when the individual becomes explicitly aware of his task and tries to put it into words. This explicit contemplation of our life, of our task in life, is essential; otherwise we run the risk of thinking we should be doing something else which is not our particular task at all. In prayer the individual comes to be aware of the whole within which he is located. Where such express elements of prayer cease to be present, life begins to lose in depth, clarity and forward movement. This is quite irrespective of what form these elements of prayer should take. In the past prayer not infrequently had a life of its own, a separate identity. It became a little world apart. Special times for prayer, special places for prayer; lots of set phrases and formulas. As a result it was not always clear what the connection between prayer and ordinary life was.

So it is misleading for us to speak of our 'prayer life' as something alongside our 'religious life', 'family life' and so on. If we regard prayer as an expression in words, an articulation, of our life's task, a way of shedding light on the situation we find ourselves in and of mapping out the direction in which we should move, then the connection between prayer and life is obvious enough.

Not a barrage of words

Prayer is not primarily a matter of our talking to God. There is no need for us to try and interest God in our affairs. A splendid instance of that is the prayer which the priests of Baal aimed at their god in the days of Elijah. In the end they get so mad that they do not know what to do next. Then Elijah mocks them:

33

'Why don't you call louder? He must be day-dreaming or busy working or away somewhere. Perhaps he is dozing and will have to be woken up.' That is precisely what prayer is *not* about. In Matthew's Gospel we read: 'In your prayers do not babble as the pagans do, for they think that by using many words they will make themselves heard. Do not be like them. Your father knows what you need before you ask Him' (Matthew 6:7–8).

A substantial part of prayer might be defined as being prepared, being on the alert, the quietness that is a prelude to a right understanding, attention, expecting and looking out for the coming of the Kingdom. Thus prayer has its place in the centre of life; and this can be seen very clearly in the life of Jesus. At crucial moments in his life, when there was an important step to be taken, we read again and again that he 'went apart to pray'. Rooted in the quietness of prayer, the right decision can come to fruition. Prepossessions fade away. Despondency and frustration are overcome.

Time and again the point is that the issues posed for us by the situation should be borne in upon us. At this juncture you may be wondering: there is all this talk about our 'task' which has to arise out of the situation; but what *is* this task, what really are the questions at issue here? We find them planted, I think, at the very beginning of the Bible: the question to Adam, who goes into hiding, who dare not accept responsibility for his actions: *Adam, where are you?* And then the question to Cain, who murdered his brother: *Where is your brother?* Questions as to a man's proper and distinctive place and his responsibility for other men; questions to which we must always be giving a fresh answer.

We have used expressions like 'reflecting on our situation', having 'a view of our life and of our task in it'. What now remains of the familiar definition of prayer as conversation with God? I said before that what God does he does through us. It is in our efforts, our exertion, that God is continually at work. The ever-changing situations in our lives signify God's way of speaking to us. Prayer is the echo of God's voice in our lives. It is a real conversation: a way of giving thanks (because our existence as such is a gift) and also of asking (because our existence is a task to be performed). Prayer even has the typical features of a conversation.

Talking is a process of speaking up and speaking out in someone's presence, a moving out from ourselves in order subsequently to return enriched. It is the same with prayer. Something happens inside us. Prayer is an expecting, an awaiting. Desire and longing are essential to prayer : a sense of the incomplete, of imperfection, and a dreaming of what has still to be. It embodies in words what we have to do and what we are as yet unable to achieve. It is a battle with fatalism, with the feeling of impotence that is always surfacing within us. What a godsend it would be to many people if they could pray, if they could let themselves go and could feel that they truly belong within a larger whole.

Thy will be done

I would like to try and say something about petitionary prayer and the question of its being answered. As I was saying earlier on : in every situation as it occurs in our lives we have to discover God's voice, his presence, his nearness to us and around us, his spirit. For that spirit is certainly there; and we have to be always laying ourselves open to it in prayer. This spirit, this 'mind', is the highest gift a man can pray for. It is what Jesus prayed for; and he was filled with it and by it. It enabled him to be in control of every situation as it arose. Prayer for this spirit is expressed magnificently in Luke 11. The passage constitutes a single whole. We often tend to lift odd bits and pieces out of it; so I want to quote it now in full. Notice particularly the dénouement at the end, where the whole thing reaches its climax.

> 'Now once he was in a certain place praying, and when he had finished one of his disciples said, "Lord, teach us to pray, just as John taught his disciples." He said to them, "Say this when you pray :
>
> > Father, may your name be held holy,
> > your kingdom come;
> > give us each day our daily bread,
> > and forgive us our sins,
> > for we ourselves forgive each one who is in debt to us.
> > And do not put us to the test."

He also said to them, "Suppose one of you has a friend and goes to him in the middle of the night to say, My friend, lend me three loaves, because a friend of mine on his travels has just arrived at my house and I have nothing to offer him; and the man answers from inside the house, Do not bother me. The door is bolted now, and my children and I are in bed; I cannot get up to give it you." I tell you, if the man does not get up and give it him for friendship's sake, persistence will be enough to make him get up and give his friend all he wants.

'So I say to you: Ask, and it will be given to you; search, and you will find; knock, and the door will be opened to you. For the one who asks always receives; the one who searches always finds; the one who knocks will always have the door opened to him. What father among you would hand his son a stone when he asked for bread? Or hand him a snake instead of a fish? Or hand him a scorpion if he asked an egg? If you then, who are evil, know how to give your children what is good, how much more will the heavenly Father give the Holy Spirit to those who ask him?'

You will be wondering: is this holy spirit, this right spirit, all that we can ask for? Is the only possible prayer: not my will, but yours be done? Yes, indeed; that is the only prayer. All other prayers are bound to be elaborations on that one. Or to put it another way: prayer is not about 'having' but about 'being', about 'well-being'. The whole point about prayer is to assimilate and come to terms in our lives with what has happened and to extend lines into the future, in a way consonant with God's purpose. It means being able to accept what we were unable to foresee.

Take, for instance, the case of an incurable disease. A recurrent tragedy. In such a case the individual concerned must learn to accept his situation and live it out as a free human being. To ask for a cure is not the right sort of prayer. Much more to the point is learning to understand the situation, laying oneself open to the spirit which even in this forlorn circumstance does not leave a man to his own devices but enables him to master his situation and not succumb to it. We may remind ourselves here of Jesus in the Garden of Olives. First of his prayer: Father, if it is possible, let this cup pass from me. That is how we must all begin. And then he comes to that tremendous prayer: not my will but yours be done. That is the process—the process of growth—which we have to undergo time and time again.

I would not wish to say that praying to be cured of this incurable disease is therefore wrong. But it must grow, surely, into that second prayer. Only then, one might say, does our necessity teach us the way of real prayer.

We can see this happening, for instance, at Lourdes, over and over again. People go there to recover their health. What is emphasized is the gift; so that prayer is often seen as one factor alongside other factors. When they get back from Lourdes, usually the ailment has not been cured. But we frequently see that they have been reconciled to their situation, they are able to accept it with a degree of inner tranquillity. They have discovered God's spirit. Their prayer has passed out of having into being.

A fire that warms

Praying for ourselves and for others is a form of asking. It is at that level. If you ask for something, you are expressing a need and you show yourself prepared to receive. But to attain the desired goal more is required than simply asking. Asking is just one part of a more comprehensive process. What are we doing, for instance, when we pray for peace in Vietnam? For a long time we have been used to think of it in terms of 'us *down here* praying to God *up there*'. And he in his turn will intervene in what is happening in Vietnam—or not. This you might envisage, more or less, as a sort of triangular relationship; but the idea is a dangerous one, because God is not stationed at the apex of this particular triangle. He works through us. We are allowed to be co-workers with God in bringing about the Kingdom of peace. The chief motive force of our prayer must be a love for the other person. When we base our praying on this attitude, we give expression to the fact that God loves and cares for that other person, that we have faith in that person's potential for good. We should not regard prayer as one factor alongside other factors. Our prayer does not exert its effect via all sorts of mysterious and elusive channels; nor should we presume to think that we can somehow change God's mind. It is we who must change. We have to be filled with the right spirit. Then our prayer will be like a stone when it has been tossed into water. From the still centre there emanate a series of circles covering a large surface. The person praying turns them into waves. In so far as the right spirit makes us a true source or centre our prayer has visible results.

We often find that our prayer is totally unproductive. That may be because it was not a prayer for the right spirit; or perhaps we did no more than pray, when we could have done so many other things. The younger generation will say : you shouldn't pray; you'd do much better to go and demonstrate. That is very likely their way of reacting to what they see in *us*. For us, prayer is quite often a free-wheeling activity that leads nowhere. So long as you just pray you have no need to show your hand, to take sides. Now the reaction of these youngsters is understandable but at the same time dangerous. Demonstrating is no substitute for praying. It may well go hand in hand with it. Pray and act. Otherwise there is a very real danger that all our activity will prove abortive because we end up feeling frustrated and embittered, or simply because we run out of steam and begin to feel more and more impotent. A praying person keeps open all the possibilities, in spite of everything. He is all the time reminding himself that he can make a go of it, that there is a way.

Of course, a great many questions remain : questions about set forms of prayer, communal prayer, the value of our praying for the departed, and so on. Still, I hope that in the context of the perspective I have attempted to provide for you, you will be able to get some way with these problems—by taking this background as a basis for *action*.

5 'The good news that Jesus is the Messiah' *(Acts 5)*

The record concerning Jesus

In what has been said so far I have tried to broach the mystery that we call God—a mystery that affects and fills our lives at the deepest level. I have also tried to show that a change in the way we speak *of* God entails a change in the way we speak *with* him. Now I would like to say something about Jesus, whom we call the Christ.

His name is frequently on our lips. But is he really a living person for us? Does he set the pattern for our living? We are coming out of a period when Jesus had features so divine that they obscured his humanity. We can see at the moment another picture of Jesus emerging, a more human picture; and this is giving rise to a different relationship with the person of Jesus. You have only to look back at the old catechisms. So many of the expressions we find in them strike us now as old-fashioned, a kind of language we no longer use, that is not real to us, so that we cannot make it our own. Jesus has become more human for us. He has come closer to us—and for two reasons in particular. First of all, we have begun to read the Gospel accounts of Jesus from a different standpoint. And then we have come to think about the relationship of God and man in a quite different way. These two factors are closely connected. Because of them, people in our day and age are able to encounter Jesus as an irresistible and inspiring person.

Let us look first at the change in how we read the Gospel accounts. We are better equipped nowadays to read the texts from which we get our information about Jesus. We know something of the aims and purposes of those who wrote them, something of the structure of their writings, and of the various ways in which they made use of language. I shall focus briefly on the person of Jesus: for, obviously, we cannot take an informed view of Jesus unless we have some understanding of the texts that give us the evidence about him. (Much of what I am going to say may be found in the Dutch catechism, or in any scripture commentary.)

1. First, something about the origins of the gospels. The first three gospels show a marked resemblance to each other, and in fact they depend on each other. Mark's gospel was written first, about the year 63 or even later. Matthew and Luke both drew on his gospel, and probably also had at their disposal a written collection of the sayings of Jesus. John's gospel was written much later, and differs greatly from the first three.

These facts are important. What they mean is that a fairly long period of time passed after the death of Jesus before accounts of his life took written form. The first written accounts form the basis on which his life was represented and proclaimed. The gospels came into being in different parts of the Holy Land. Each particular place had its own tradition, and its own way of proclaiming the message of Jesus, reflecting the needs of the people in that area, and the historical period.

2. This growth of the proclamation concerning Jesus came about in distinct stages, step by step, as it were. We can point to, roughly speaking, three layers. The *first* and oldest layer consists in the message that he who was crucified is now alive. God has raised him up. He is risen. This is the object of the testimony. He is alive. Only gradually did it become necessary to expand the message somewhat. People who had not known Jesus particularly well were asking: All right, but *who* is alive? What did he in fact say and do? And so a *second* layer emerged: the words and deeds of Jesus.

And out of that same firm conviction that he is alive there eventually arises yet a *third* layer: the accounts of Jesus' birth and boyhood. Understandably, the oldest layer—Jesus is alive—tallies pretty closely in all four gospels.

In the second layer—the sayings and deeds of Jesus—there are considerable differences between the gospel writers. The third layer—Jesus' birth and boyhood—is even less of an entity, when you compare one story with another. Only Matthew and Luke include an account of Jesus' birth and early years. These stories stand at the beginning of their respective gospels; yet this (third) layer was the last to emerge. The significance of the infancy stories is not that they give us an exact account of everything connected with the birth of Jesus exactly as it happened. This is not journalistic reportage. It is a message about Jesus. The function of these stories is to underline the importance of the life of Jesus. You must make you own comparison between the stories of the birth of Jesus in Matthew and in Luke: you will soon see that they don't have much in common. The point in each narrative is its message, its inner meaning. For Matthew, who wrote for a Jewish audience, it was necessary to show that Jesus came, like the old people of God, out of Egypt. Luke wrote for a non-Jewish audience, and he wanted to draw attention to Jesus' birth in a stable, among shepherds, the outcasts of society. So the two gospel writers proclaim, as believers, their own particular ways of regarding Jesus.

3.   The purpose of the gospels *is not to relate history but to convey a message*; we should not read them as biographies, designed to give us a detailed account of the events of Jesus' life from birth to death. Their whole point is the message that Jesus lives and that through him that prospect is open to us all. We must therefore keep trying to grasp what it is that the evangelists are wanting to convey to us with their sometimes strange and wonderful stories.

We are quite differently constituted from the people for whom the evangelists were writing. We invariably ask : is it true or not? Did it really happen or not? If it did not happen exactly as it says, we do not waste any more time over it. Take, for instance, the story of Jesus being tempted in the wilderness. Very likely it did not happen literally in that particular way. But that in no way detracts from the tremendous reality it serves to express. What we have to keep asking is : what is it they want to get over to us in their stories? What kind of language are they using : poetic, didactic, reporting, etcetera?

In the old catechisms and the old way of teaching religion, it was taken for granted that everything recorded about Jesus happened literally in the way it is written down. Sometimes quite disparate levels of reality are involved. So, for example, we were taught that God the Son took a human soul and a human body, took to himself the nature of man; that Jesus was born at Bethlehem; that he fasted for forty days and nights in the desert and was tempted by the devil; that he died on the cross and his soul descended into limbo; that Jesus himself united his soul with his body and rose immortal and glorified from the unopened tomb.

When we try to rediscover what the gospel-writers were really getting at, we find ourselves closer to a much more human Jesus. A Jesus who is not made remote from us by all those highly miraculous features. The life of Jesus is not 'miraculous'. It is a marvel of humanity. It is no accident, therefore, that resistance is making itself felt nowadays against an excessively literal view of the events of his life. I need only mention the discussions going on about the virgin birth. But to go into that in any detail would carry us too far afield.

4.   Finally, it is not without importance that we are beginning to realize more clearly how impossible it is to understand Jesus apart from the background provided by the Old Testament. And that is what we have nearly always tried to do. Without the Old Testament we cannot understand a single term used by the evangelists in their attempts to denote this marvellous person, Jesus. Always they turn back to the Old Testament to find models that will help them to shed light on Jesus' life. Indispensable to the account of his temptation in the wilderness is the background provided by the journey of the Jewish people through the wilderness. The story of the transfiguration on Mount Tabor can only be read with the life of Moses in mind (Exodus 34:9 ff.). Many other examples might be mentioned.

Even Jesus himself interpreted his own person entirely in terms of the Old Testament. We might say that in Jesus God became more visible than ever before. But Jesus can only experience and express this in continuity with the way God had made himself known in the Old Testament. Jesus sees his own life more and more sharply reflected in the suffering servant of Yahweh, about whom the prophet Isaiah had spoken with such fervour (e.g. Isaiah 53).

Jesus, a marvel of humanity

Running right through the whole of Jewish history is a single great expectation: the advent or coming of the Messiah. That expectation is given verbal expression in a variety of ways. The main one, of course, we find in the book of the prophet Isaiah. In his songs about the Servant of Yahweh you can feel the intensity of this expectation (Isaiah 42:1–7; 49:1–9; 52:13 to 53:12; 35:5–6; 61). The Messiah is he who will one day make salvation a reality; who will establish the long-expected *shalom*; who will bring about the new covenant between God and his people. He will be God-with-men. Then men will melt down their weapons into ploughshares. On the basis of his solidarity with Yahweh, this Servant of Yahweh will live for people 'even unto death'. Jesus came increasingly to recognize himself in this Servant. The apostles and the first Christians also acknowledged Jesus in that role. But not the majority of Jews. They found it farcical when the characteristics of the Messiah were ascribed to Jesus. Just imagine! the son of a carpenter! They were unable to believe that God could go to the extreme of becoming a man. The fact is, we too have a great deal of difficulty with the same thing. Consequently, the Jews are still waiting for the Messiah. That is why every Jewish family that celebrates the Passover meal keeps one chair symbolically empty. The circle is not yet completed. Someone is still absent.

Perhaps I may be allowed at this point to cite one of the oldest testimonies regarding Jesus. It is a passage in Acts (5:34–42). What captivates me in this passage is the unbounded enthuiasm the apostles feel for the person of Jesus and also the terse summing up of the whole 'glad tidings': Jesus is the Messiah. These four words tell us everything. Not a word needs to be added. With them the New Testament is complete. For this message the disciples went through the fire. They were prepared to stake their lives on it. We say, with a shrug of the shoulders: 'Is *that* what all the fuss is about? So what!' But that is because we are not Jews and so can have little idea of the total resonance of that word 'Messiah'. The event I am talking about took place soon after Jesus' death. The movement centred around Jesus was spreading so rapidly that it was making considerable inroads into the official Jewish religion. A stop had to be put to it. The apostles were arrested and brought before the council. The story goes on :

> 'One member of the Sanhedrin, however, a Pharisee called Gamaliel, who was a doctor of the Law and respected by the whole people, stood up and asked to have the men taken outside for a time. Then he addressed the Sanhedrin, "Men of Israel, be careful how you deal with these people. There was Theudas who became notorious not so long ago. He claimed to be someone important, and he even collected about four hundred followers; but when he was killed, all his followers scattered and that was the end of them. And then there was Judas the Galilean, at the time of the census, who attracted crowds of supporters; but he got killed too, and all his followers dispersed. What I suggest, therefore, is that you leave these men alone and let them go. If this enterprise, this movement of theirs, is of human origin it will break up of its own accord; but if it does in fact come from God you will . . . be unable to destroy them. . . ." His advice was accepted; and they had the apostles called in, gave orders for them to be flogged, warned them not to speak in the name of Jesus and released them. And so they left the presence of the Sanhedrin glad to have had the honour of suffering humiliation for the sake of the name. They preached every day both in the Temple and in private houses and their proclamation . . . [of the good news that Jesus is the Messiah] was never interrupted.'

What tremendous enthusiasm! And all because Jesus is the Messiah. We keep coming across echoes in the gospels of the Servant-of-Yahweh songs from Isaiah. Luke makes Jesus' official ministry start in the synagogue at Nazareth, his home town (4:16–30). Jesus registers his presence there in a manner that could not possibly be misunderstood. He opens up the scroll containing the book of Isaiah and reads aloud a passage from one of the Servant of Yahweh songs, adding : 'This text is being fulfilled today, even as you listen.' The result? He barely managed to reach safety. What arrogance, what presumption! Yet Jesus made no claims. Inevitably, it spoke for itself. John the Baptist in prison begins to have doubts and sends to Jesus to ask : 'Are you the one who is to come, or must we wait for someone else?' (Luke 7:18–23). Jesus' only reply is: Look at what is happening: 'the blind see again, the lame walk, lepers are cleansed, and the deaf hear, the dead are raised to life, the Good News is proclaimed to the poor. . . .' And these very things were the marks of the Servant in Isaiah's prophecy. Jesus lives as the Messiah. He lives for the happiness of others. The Gospel depicts him as a person who fascinated everyone, whom no one could disregard. Perhaps the most characteristic thing about his life is the authority with which he acts: a natural authority enabling him to dominate the situations in which he finds himself. They do not get him down. He does not dodge the difficulties. He does not shuffle thorny questions off on to other people. He does not compromise in order to keep his hands clean. He is straightforward in his behaviour. He simply does what he thinks has to be done: assuming the role of the Servant of Yahweh to the very end. Because he has this firm link with Yahweh he finds the strength to stand up for justice and freedom.

If laws gave rise to an inhuman situation, he broke them. Even bonds of kinship are relative, so far as he is concerned: 'They are my mother and my brothers who do the will of my Father.' He set out to break down the walls between men. The people particularly receptive to his message are those whom society most tends to ignore: 'ordinary' people with no pretensions, without a knowledge of the law of Moses; people who were not really taken seriously, who were more or less without rights. Theirs is an open attitude; and so Jesus prefers to address himself to them —to the great annoyance of the 'right-minded ones'.

Jesus sets people on the right way when they have strayed from it, he gives people a future. There is a superb example of that in the story of the woman taken in adultery (John 8). The pharisees want to trap Jesus; so they bring to him a woman who has committed adultery. According to the law, therefore, she must be stoned. On the one side are the pharisees, who put the law above all else and so are themselves in danger of becoming more and more stern and inhuman. With a simple saying Jesus sets them back upon the way that has a future: 'If there is one of you who has not sinned let him be the first to throw a stone at her.' An address to the conscience that causes the humanity in them to begin to unfreeze once more. They leave in silence. And on the other side stands the woman. According to them she has slipped and fallen. She has ignored the most fundamental norms. Jesus does not condemn her; nor does he pry into what she has done. She too can proceed along a road that has a future.

A different assessment?

I said that Jesus did what he believed had to be done: taking upon himself the role of the Servant of Yahweh to the very end. And that means he lived a life of calm and obedience, a life of total surrender, in an intense and binding relationship with Yahweh. This was the source of his strength, of his power to live for others, and especially for the well-being of those who had very little good fortune in their lives. Thus he took his stand for justice and freedom wherever those values were in danger of being trampled underfoot. When I was talking at the beginning of this book about our experience of God, I made the point that the more an individual is able to meet the demands of his calling, the more he becomes himself, the more God becomes visible in him. I then tried to exemplify this by means of figures like Moses and Jacob, but also by reference to our own experiences. If God was already visible in such figures as Jacob and Moses, in Jesus God has come as it were tangibly among us. Jesus was himself, as no one else has ever been. He fathomed and, in his living, experienced the deepest potentialities of our existence. That is why from the earliest times we Christians have affirmed that in Jesus God has fully revealed himself. His whole life is buoyed up by this loving and powerful presence. Moses was permitted to use the name 'Yahweh' to denote this mystery. The name signifies: 'I will be (there)', 'I will not let go of you'. In Jesus this Yahweh has acquired an unforgettable face. For more than anyone else Jesus was close to people. He never rejected anybody, never let anybody go. Therefore 'God raised him high and gave him the name which is above all other names' (Philippians 2:9).

The various titles used in the New Testament with reference to Jesus are attempts to define this marvellous figure in words. But each name points more or less in the same direction. Whether Jesus is called Son of David, Son of God, Son of Man or Messiah, these are all Jewish titles referring to the person on whom all the Jews had centred their expectations—names indicating the closest possible connection with Yahweh, names awakening the hope that this fulness of life will be to the benefit of all. Significantly enough, we are not called after the name of Jesus but by the name which has become the characteristic expression for Jesus: Messiah, a name rendered in Greek as *Christos*: the anointed One, the One sent.

This way of assessing Jesus will be unfamiliar to some of you. For we have been taught to regard what is special about Jesus as residing more especially in the fact that at a moment determined by the Father he was born out of heaven; that he descended straight from heaven to earth without much connection with all that had been on the earth up to that time, in other words, as something totally alien in this terrestrial scene. He lived here a number of years and after his death returned to the heaven whence he had come. The evangelists tried to express the enormous significance of Jesus with these images, which fitted into their world view. The real issue is not the images themselves but what they were meant to signify.

When it came to what was so extraordinary about Jesus our attitude was really based on considerations of this sort: Jesus is not to be compared with us. He came down from heaven, he is the Son of God. That is also why he could work miracles and why he was able to rise again. Our age requires of us, I believe, that we should learn to tread the same path as Jesus' contemporaries were obliged to tread. All that they saw was a human being, Jesus, from Nazareth. But a person who generated warmth and captivated people, who cast the spell of his authority over them. Or else he roused fierce hostility. But you couldn't ignore him. What is special about Jesus, therefore, is not that he came down from heaven and has gone back there, but that he made such an overwhelming impression that people came to speak of him in that fashion. We might also put it like this: Jesus is not great and unique because he is the Son of God; but we have come to acknowledge Jesus as Son of God because the life he lived was so splendid and so unique. The aspect of uniqueness is precisely encapsulated in the name 'Messiah', which I keep returning to. But yet another factor plays a part in our relationship with Jesus. It's not simply that we used to start at the other end: Jesus was God and so was able to act as he did. Another contributory factor was that competition between God and man which I have mentioned several times already. That whole way of thinking made it very difficult to see Jesus as a single person. One got the idea that Jesus was a person made up of two component parts which simply could not be held together: God and man. The entire history of Christianity represents God and man as embroiled in a fierce, competitive struggle with each other in Jesus.

Where the emphasis has been placed on Jesus being the Son of God, his being man has disappeared completely from view; and where Jesus has been regarded primarily as man, there has almost inevitably been a denial of his being God. Especially in the first five centuries this was *the* subject of debate. Yet God and man do not operate on different planes. As we have seen, God works through human beings.

In our own encounter with religion the fact is that Jesus' being as man has been obliterated by his being as God. Jesus knew everything, could do anything, and so on. Thus he became a figure so remote from us that any emulation of Jesus on our part was felt to be an impossible task. After all, there was no field in which you could measure up to Jesus. He had absolutely no weaknesses because he was God. Represented in this way Jesus impinges upon us less and less, because this notion of things, where we are concerned, does not do justice to Jesus' person. What we are seeing in our time, therefore, is the growth of a different way of envisaging Jesus; and at the same time there is a shift in our association with Jesus. At one time it was a state of being bound together in an intimate contact, a strong sense of piety, the expression of which was centred more especially around the eucharist. The business of nuns being 'brides of Christ' sprang out of the same atmosphere. Now we are feeling our way toward a different relationship with Jesus, our brother, toward a life lived in his spirit, a continuous process of being urged forward by his inspiration, a living in the wake of his spirit of service. Jesus is pointing away from himself nowadays toward the world and its suffering. Thus many a Christian is experiencing his relation to the Lord as a believer more as a command to enter the world with the Lord's spirit than as a way of running to him for refuge out of the world. It is a clear difference of emphasis.

The main question in all this is not: so what distinguishes Jesus from Buddha, from Mohammed or from Martin Luther King? One could go on and on discussing that—it is all quite pointless. It does not get to the heart of the matter. The point is not what Jesus signifies in general, but what he signifies for you, for me. What is it that Jesus really means to us? Why do we so seldom mention him in the affairs of daily life? Why does he so seldom set a pattern for us when difficult decisions confront us in our lives? Is he a unique person for us, as our husband or our wife is unique? Is Jesus a force where we are concerned? Does he bring quietness and calm into our lives? Something to take hold of? A sense of assurance? Does his person tell us that everything, our own life, does after all make sense? Or does Jesus make us restless? An unrest, for instance, that marked the apostles and the disciples? Does he keep up on the alert, so that instead of dozing off we remain ready for the fray and open in respect of the things that are to come? How do we react to his plea: 'Could none of you stay awake with me one hour?' (Matthew 26:40).

6 The church an on-going process

The new orientation of our thinking and of the way we live naturally finds a counterpart in our experience of being the church. To say something briefly about the church is not a simple task. The more so because what is going on in the Catholic church nowadays has deep roots in the past.* A very closed church is being rather roughly prised open as a result of current developments in society. And none of us can say exactly where all this is leading. A great deal of what is happening now, in the life of the church and in religion generally, is not in fact of our own choosing; so it would be a sign of unrealistic optimism to cheer at everything that happens and put out the flags to give it a welcome. We have been caught unawares, to some extent, by the times we live in. As members both of society and of the church we find ourselves in quite different circumstances from those in which most of us were brought up. And we need to know just where we are with this situation. Nor does that mean that we should follow uncritically in the wake of every innovation or that we must reject whatever is new as somehow inferior. We are faced with the question of what the church's mandate is in this day and age.

The question is a hard one. We therefore have to be on our guard against facile answers and speciously attractive talk. Nor is there much sense in setting up a whole network of new structures without having some clue as to which direction the church of today should be moving in. I cannot project for you a complete picture of tomorrow's church. How could I? So it seems

* The author writes particularly of the Dutch Catholic Church. But his remarks apply generally.

to me best if I draw up a list, point by point, of a number of factors that have a part to play in the process of renewal now engaging the church.

The situation in which we as the church find ourselves can be nicely illustrated by the following two statements, each made at the opening of a new parish : they are not very far separated from each other in time, but as regards mental outlook there is a great gulf between them. It is typical of our situation that the two possible 'styles' of experience occur side by side : and that so many of us feel that we are standing with one foot in the old situation and the other in the new way of 'being the church'. The two statements are taken from the records of the diocese of Haarlem; in each, it is the bishop speaking :

November 1963:
'Your pastor finds himself confronted in this new parish with a very onerous task in the cure of souls. We trust that through their *submissiveness* and united co-operation the faithful will make their utmost contribution *to the prosperity of their own parish* and will also help according to their means to alleviate the financial burdens of the church council. May the parishioners by their piety and their Christian living *gratify their pastor to the full,* so that he *may shepherd them* with joy and not in sadness *to their true happiness.*'

(Note the words in italics !)

January 1967:
'Thousands of people will be living in this new town, whose building is already well on its way to completion. Some people have moved in already, and they are expecting to settle down, establish their homes here, and lead a good, enjoyable existence. They are hoping to find here a situation and a way of life that is attractive and conducive to happiness. It is precisely because we believe that by command of Christ the church has a task to fulfil in this respect that we want to belong to the church. With the proclamation of Jesus Christ as its starting-point, the church must help people grow toward greater happiness, greater peace, a greater degree of reconciliation. Inspired by the gospel, it has

51

to serve society so that the individual person may grow freer, happier and more human. . . .'

You notice the difference?

A different view of the world

The very different attitude people take toward the world these days is of crucial importance to what is now going on in the church. Nowadays we talk of the world in a very positive way; we are no longer resigned to it as a wicked and dangerous place; we don't want just to steer a course through it as through a necessary evil. This world is precious to us. I am not saying it is good. That would scarcely be realistic. But we know very well that it could be different. And there, precisely there, our task lies. The person who expects nothing of this life, who is resigned to all the wretchedness that exists, is in danger of putting off his hope of happiness to the next world, to the hereafter. That is what happened, by and large, in times past. It was not really until technology began to make itself felt in the course of the last century that this attitude began to change. People began to take an interest in the natural world and its potential. Of course, they had always been interested in it; but it had been largely a philosophic interest, and hadn't led to much effort to alter the world or to make it a better place to live in.

That is where Karl Marx (1818–1883) and people like him come in. Marx argued that people want to run away from reality, they want to draw a veil over the real state of affairs which is wretched and evil. That is why they have turned to religion, to project a better world in the next life. But this is not right. We must make the real world such that people will no longer need to dream about a better reality.

In the same period came Charles Darwin (1809–1882) with the concept of evolution, a dynamic view of reality which was to spread further and further and enjoy an unprecedented popularity through the work of Teilhard de Chardin.

We can safely say that because of the growing influence of science and technology man today is much concerned with the future. He is banking on a better future. The number of people specializing in the physical or behavioural sciences and in technology is always on the increase. We talk these days about 'global construction' or 'world development', about 'furthering the well-being of all people'. These are ideas that could only have emerged in our own time. Modern man can no longer deduce the pattern of his existence exclusively from the past. Tradition has ceased to play the dominant role which until very recently it occupied. Within the church, as in society as a whole, something like a 'sacred' tradition was, after all, the governing factor.

Our whole life is now geared to a dynamic orientated on the future.

If the church wants to maintain its credibility, then it must live out and propagate its message within this altered context. To talk of a glorious future ahead of us is only plausible if the evidence for that future is being formed here and now, and if that future is to some extent already beginning to dawn.

In point of fact that is the very core of the New Testament message. Jesus gives to his disciples to do what he himself does. Their mandate is to proclaim that the Kingdom of God is at hand (there is a future, things are going somewhere, it all makes sense). But at the same time they must establish here and now the signs and tokens of that ultimate *Shalom*, that kingdom, that final deliverance: their mandate is to exorcise and expel the powers that hold man prisoner and to cure the sick of their ailments. Only if that Kingdom is already leaving positive traces of its presence is our speaking of it more than hollow, empty talk. Believing in a God who will not let us go should not paralyse us, but on the contrary stir us into action.

From island refuge to launching-pad

In an earlier cultural period the church's role was that of an island refuge, an oasis, an asylum. Protection from an evil world. For in the world there was no salvation. Anybody who remained outside the barque of Peter was lost for good in the surging ocean billows of this world. The directive issued by the Dutch bishops in 1954 was a sort of terminal convulsion of that mental outlook. A solemn warning of the perils which outside the church lurk menacingly in every quarter (radio, newspapers, politics and so forth). Nowadays the church must be much more a point of reorientation, of reflective reasoning, stimulus and encouragement. And a source of inspiration that will enable us to carry out our mandate, in spite of setbacks and opposition. The church is very much turned outward. In this new orientation the sacraments too have quite a different role to play. For instance, the inspiration deriving from the eucharist must no longer be allowed to serve primarily to perpetuate an attitude of partial resignation to the affairs of life. On the contrary, that inspiration must lead to making the climate of living more liveable and if necessary to taking steps and implementing active measures to change it.

A great degree of openness will be needed, a concentrated attention to everything that is going on, if we want to catch on to what our task is.

Well-being, 'salvation', is not a cut-and-dried proposition, so that all we have to do is to share it out. We have to prospect for it, search it out, designate it; which is also why in referring to the church nowadays we prefer to use a somewhat more dynamic term : the people of God. The phrase in itself evokes for us a picture of the Jewish people journeying through the wilderness. The fact that we like to use this name shows how we ourselves envisage and experience what it is to be the church. The phrase 'People of God' expresses the dynamic, questing, provisional character which is coming more and more to prevail in the church. It is a situation where the tent is more appropriate than any imposing temple. Thus the use nowadays of terms like 'shaping church', 'creating church', instead of plain 'church'. You cannot in fact say that the church *is*; the church happens, the church is engendered from age to age. All the organizations, structures and councils that we set up, all the techniques we learn, have in themselves extraordinarily little to do with 'creating the church.' We can only hope that they will be good conductors of this dynamic process of becoming-the-church. However fine structures may be, they cannot guarantee that 'it' will happen. Certainly not when structures or traditions come to play such a restrictive role that spontaneity and charisma are hemmed in and dammed up.

Unlimited openness to the outside

This considerable openness, this turning outward, has helped us shed a certain amount of complacency ('the prosperity of one's own parish'). The questing attitude that is now beginning to predominate spells the end of the sort of mentality that would claim to have a monopoly of truth and wisdom. We are now entering into a real dialogue with other people. No longer with the idea of separating ourselves, of fencing ourselves off from the outside. We are looking for what it is that links us with others. We are discovering that others, too, are heart and soul in the battle for a better world, even if what inspires them is at times very different. And so what we are seeing now is not only an intensive dialogue between the Christian churches. There are also conversations taking place with the other great world religions; and a dialogue is beginning to get under way with Marxism. This is a question of 'oikumene' in the broadest sense of the term: inhabited world. Here lies the church's task; here 'it' has to happen.

The church is often blamed for being too preoccupied with its own internal affairs. 'Ecclesiastical' has begun to be almost a dirty word. We must be on our guard against phobias of this sort. The man who has nothing can hardly share it with others. If the church as a community does not have a sufficient identity of its own, it can propagate little beyond its borders. The most it will achieve will be a rash and premature assimilation or rejection of this, that or the other development within society.

It is much to the point in this connection to read a passage like Matthew 10—the calling and training of the apostles—where we can watch Jesus himself occupied with 'matters ecclesiastical'. He gives a small body of men a tough training. They have to radiate inspiration. Only then can 'it' happen, only then can they 'do the signs' needed to give credibility to their words. A touch of 'personality' is engendered in the disciples that simply cannot fail to get results. So as they get out and about we see the spark spreading. Then the 'church' begins to resemble a spot of oil, spreading slowly outwards. The church is required to understand the signs of the times. That is its *first* duty—but it is also a difficult one, calling for some constant and concentrated thought. It means theoretically that we point out and stimulate such good as there is; and when we see the opposite happening, we point that out too and protest vehemently about it. This good, this well-being, will always be connected in some way with the truly human, truly decent kind of existence toward which we are moving, an existence worthy of human beings, but one which in positive terms we cannot fully envisage. And yet we sense very well if things are happening that conflict with the value and dignity of man. Then we must be there, on the spot, sometimes collectively, sometimes as individuals. With a basis of hard thinking about the gospel to sustain us, we have to be on the trail all the time, searching out what is good and what is not; and for this we need a new stance and a new direction. We need to be greatly concerned with everything that goes on in our society.

As I said earlier on, the good, the 'salvation' that we seek is no package deal that priestly hands can bring down upon the altar. Yet if we are not to be discouraged by what we have to go through, if we are to be put back again and again on the right track, if we are to know what it is we have to do, then we are bound to come together so that that simple gesture of Jesus may continually permeate our being. 'Breaking and sharing, be the impossible, do the unthinkable, dying to rise again.' Wherever this gesture is performed with intensity, there 'church' happens; where it results effectively in Christian being, there the church happens, too.

From a material standpoint the occurrence of the church, in the sense just described, is not distinguishable from what is done by others as well. The distinction lies solely in the inspiration by which the Christian operates, in the interpretation he associates with what he does.

The laborious process of growing toward a shared responsibility

Within the process now going forward another factor of major significance is the shift taking place in the functioning of authority. Authority depends less and less on the position a person occupies or on the fact of having been 'put in authority'. It is coming to be associated with the inspiration which a person is able to offer, with the trust which people feel they can place in somebody. Authority comes from exercising persuasion, giving a lead; but people will not let anybody simply tell them what to do, unless at the same time they have a sense of confidence and inspiration in him.

Along with a change in the functioning of authority has come an obvious shift in the way authority operates, the measures it adopts. The notion of duty, which predominated for so long, even within the life of the church, is being progressively replaced by the appeal to private conscience, to personal responsibility. This change is proving too sudden for many people. 'Out on a limb' is beginning to have a typically churchy ring about it; and a very different type of church person is springing up these days. The obedient church member is now starting to become an enfranchized Christian. What used to be taken care of by the law is now coming to be a matter of private option. Less and less can it be said that one is a good Catholic if one has performed one's obligations. What is more, the main sanction which helped to safeguard the law is no longer the terrible threat it once was: namely, the fear of hell. And so we see that the worth accorded to the church's hierarchy depends on the inspiration they have to offer, on the guidance and leadership they give, and not on the way in which they lay down minute rules about how we should live. Even within the church the democratizing trends now discernible everywhere are having their effect. But it is particularly difficult to organize these promptings. An unwarranted amount of time is spent nowadays on organization. The awakening of a real sense of involvement, of a readiness to belong and to be a part of it, proceeds at a very slow pace indeed. A lot of time is still needed for this business of growing toward a situation where we are answerable as a community, to and for one another.

You must want to be part of it

As a result of the new questing and outward-looking attitude and a growing sense of personal responsibility the national (and nominal) church of the past is developing into a church where membership is a matter of decision and free choice.

Karl Rahner once said : not everyone is called to the church, but everyone *is* called to the Kingdom of God. In so saying he finally relegated to the past the adage : 'outside the church there is no salvation'—and along with it the fear that possessed some people inside the church. At the same time the sacraments are lifted out of a climate of fear, too. Think of the implications for infant baptism, for instance, or for the remission of sins. Get the baby baptized as soon as possible—just imagine, if it should die without baptism! You could never forgive yourself. And if you were going on a long journey, for example, you wanted to make pretty sure of going to confession beforehand—in case anything should happen to you.

Being a believer and belonging to the church has become a much more deliberate affair. Going thoughtlessly, more or less automatically, through the motions of being a believer has become practically impossible. In the old 'tribal' church it was only too possible—you could simply drift along with it. Anybody who belongs to a church nowadays has to keep reassessing the whole time what this means to him. To let oneself be wafted along on the surface of prefabricated formulas and fixed structures is less and less possible.

This entails a shift from quantity to quality. At one time rather a lot of emphasis was put on quantity, on numbers: the number of people coming into the church. The more souls, the more rejoicing. Then, too, it was easy to become a member of that church. The idea of quantity also came up in connection with the ministration of the sacraments. If a sacrament confers grace, why not administer the sacraments at as early an age as possible? But now we see an increasing emphasis on quality. It must take some effort to belong. The crucial thing is not numbers, but rather the involvement, the kind of concern shown by those who call themselves Christians.

You must genuinely want to belong. If you receive the sacraments, that must in fact entail an element of experience. It has to be a definite climax. It must take some effort to be a part of this church; and that effort involves the heart, not just the mind. For if it should come to an 'elite church' in that sense, then we are on the wrong path.

To talk about the church of the future is difficult. The openness continues and is increasing. The strong sense of group isolation which, in the Roman Catholic Church in predominantly Protestant countries, grew out of its position as a minority, is visibly diminishing. In every area, in every possible context, the 'RC' emphasis is diminishing: in the political sphere, the communication media, the educational system, public and social life, and so on. Everything points to the fact that the 'tribal church' phase is now at an end. By the look of things, there will emerge more and more small groups of committed Christians. It is some years since Harvey Cox first pointed this out. In his brief but compelling book, *God's Revolution and Man's Responsibility*, he argues that the church, to be the church, must model itself to some extent on a 'guerilla' pattern. A small mobile group which meets regularly to talk things over and gain encouragement, then disperses so that each member can carry out his individual task, then comes together again, and so on. A group of Dutch students for Theology and Pastoral Ministry have put it like this:

'In our view certain groups (and we intend to be such a group) are going to emerge, which, drawn together around the word of Christ and inspired by his call to deliverance, want to get to grips with society. They will want to try and achieve unity between the theory and practice of their belief, and to live out their faith as a liberation of the individual person, oppressed as he is by present-day social conditions and structures. They will want to be action groups, aimed at exposing and opposing social injustice. . . . They cannot believe in Christ's word without as a logical result of that attacking power and property structures that make the human person a pawn, a factor in economic production, a consumer-animal . . . (and that they intend to achieve) by consistently refusing to accommodate themselves, by maintaining a critical distance from things as they are. And by conducting information campaigns and activities of that sort they will try and induce others to take the same attitude. . . . Unity, solidarity and universality are no longer for us terms that apply within the church; they apply to society. For us *oikoumene* means . . . the way all people live together: one world or no world. It must be obvious that by constituting ourselves as we have, we have made ourselves into peripheral figures and marginal groups.'

This is the tone adopted by one of these groups. More and more groups of the same kind are on their way. They may not all be marked so clearly by a spirit of social criticism; but it would be true of them all that anyone wishing to belong to them has to make a definite choice.

Of course, this way of 'being the church' can only be realized on a local basis; and that entails a high degree of decentralization. A church can no longer be governed, in the old sense of that term, from one central point, be it Archbishop's House or Rome. As I said, the function of authority must be primarily to stimulate, to give guidance and leadership and to take the gospel as a starting-point from which to frame critical questions.

Our gatherings matter

This quite different set-up has due consequences for the way we think and feel about the sacraments. I shall have more to say about this later on. The somewhat automatic, sometimes even rather magical approach to the sacraments is on its way out. The term 'inspiration' is coming to be used a great deal more than 'validity' or 'efficacy'.

Even church building itself is changing. Our new churches are an attempt to express the recently developing climate. A church should really be something of a meeting-place, a place of encounter. It no longer has to be a special sacral building; which is why more churches are coming to be used for a great variety of purposes. And now that the tribal church is disappearing, we have no further need of big churches. Again, in the majority of new church buildings it is made very obvious that the priest's position within the people of God has now changed.

So when do you belong to this church?

It is becoming less and less possible to use the habit of Sunday church attendance as the sole test of whether somebody belongs to the church or not. What is the role of the communication media in this respect? Is it more inspiring to watch the eucharist well celebrated on TV than to take part in a slovenly, uninspiring celebration in one's own parish church? When does it mean something to us to be together with a group of people inside a church? Do we feel we are united? Is the importance of this coming together of people who do not know each other somehow misrepresented? Is there more chance of 'creating the church' in smaller groups which can inspire and activate?

Another thing that gets more problematical is the criterion of orthodoxy (correct thinking in matters of doctrine). For a long time this was taken to show whether somebody was of the right persuasion or not—but this is determined nowadays less on grounds of doctrine, more in terms of how a person lives. Of course, orthodoxy is still necessary, up to a point; but orthopraxy (the right kind of doing, right way of living) is now just as important and crucial a yardstick.

Orthodoxy in matters of doctrine should be a means to a genuinely Christian way of behaviour. Otherwise the 'truth' element becomes unduly isolated and traditional formularies get the whole life of the church in a stranglehold. What we are seeing is a shift from the principle of 'truth' to that of 'truthfulness', authenticity—and not only in the church, but in society as a whole.

Assertions of truth, declarations of dogma, accusations of heresy on doctrinal grounds are less and less able to shield the church of Christ from a lack or loss of authenticity. Orthopraxy is a very ancient criterion, anyway. The first Christians were approved by the people as a whole because of the way in which they lived (Acts 2:47).

Practical assistance
I began this chapter by setting side by side the two passages from the records of the Diocese of Haarlem. They illustrate a contrast. I then noted, point by point, a number of important topics that come into every discussion on being the church. You will have noticed, of course, that the various points are closely interrelated and here and there merge into one.

I want to end as I began, with two contrasting pictures. I shall set down in two facing columns two different ways of being the church. In reality they are very extensively intertwined. We are not concerned here with giving out value-judgments, but only of ensuring that we are aware of how a quite different climate of living is bringing to life a quite different church. There is noticeably an evident shift from the first column to the second. It is causing a good deal of pain—but the pain, one hopes, is of the kind that goes hand in hand with every process of growth. (See diagram on next page.)

<table>
<tr><td>being the church: old style</td><td>being the church: new style</td></tr>
</table>

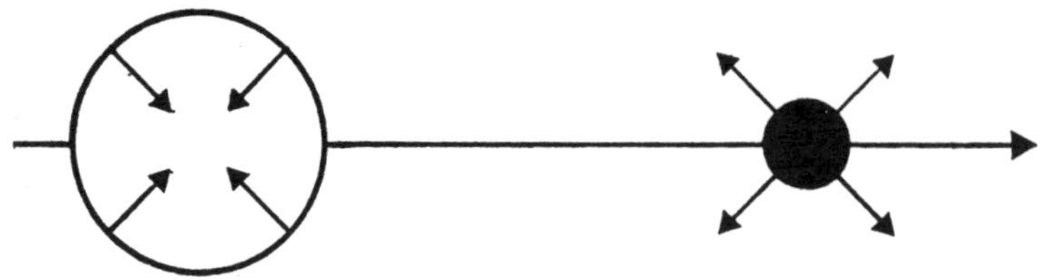

inward-looking	— outward-looking (on a basis of inspiration discovered and shared together)
worship central: validly received sacrament gives grace (sometimes a rather automatic conception, sometimes even rather magical)	— worship has a central place (must be a convincing whole. Great emphasis on proclamatory character of word and gesture)
mystical body of Christ	— people of God (dynamic, seeking, listening)
'outside the church no salvation'	— frontiers blurred (God's salvation and revelation to be found outside the church, too)
world is evil	— world is precious to us
the hereafter (strongly emphasized in combination with the above)	— en route towards a new heaven and new earth (we are banking even now on that future)
hierarchy central	— the whole people of God (democratic trends)
duty-ethics (I have done my duty)	— appeal (personal responsibility, private conscience, enfranchizement)
quantity (number of people, amount of grace; therefore sacraments to be received as early as possible)	— quality
national or 'tribal' church (inherited Christianity)	— 'voluntary' church (freely adopted Christianity)

7 Who can lead this people of God?

Effects of change on the idea of an official ministry

This is the place to say something about the position of the
official minister within the people of God; for no one who thinks
he has something to say about the exercise of the ministry at the
present time can do so unless he has some idea of the current
function of the church. And though the notes and comments in
our last chapter may be rather sketchy, all the same we have
discovered a certain trend. Look at those two columns on the
facing page. They are a rough attempt to state the difference
between the church we were brought up in and the church as
it is now in process of developing. It must be obvious that such
a major change affects the priest at the very deepest level. The
priest who fits the first column will be a very different priest
from the one who suits the second. Brought up and trained in
the old church, the priest nowadays sometimes has his back to
the wall, because things are being asked of him which he simply
cannot manage to cope with. A lot of clergy just now are going
through a difficult process of reorientation. Others are frustrated
because the changes are going forward much too slowly. Add to
that the whole range of problems centred around celibacy in the
Roman Catholic Church at the moment, and you can imagine
that the position many priests find themselves in is scarcely an
enviable one. Of course you cannot dismiss this question by
saying, as one hears said from time to time: 'They don't pray
any more, they have no faith any more.' No; these are simply
the effects of a period of transition. Meanwhile, a lot of hard
work gets done; and there is a vigorous search for ways in which

a priest today can function as a man of his time. National and diocesan clergy meetings tackle this question regularly. In the Protestant churches, too, the question of the ministry is under constant review. I will try briefly to illustrate the nature of this change with reference to what I have already said about the church, in the last chapter.

What effect has it on the priest, that the church is far more outward-looking than it used to be; that public worship is no longer directed in the first instance to giving us strength to survive in a wicked world, but to mobilize people to change the world wherever it needs changing; and that the emphasis in worship has shifted from 'validity' to inspiration? All these things make high demands on the ordained minister. He must be able to inspire a group. He has constantly to ensure that the members of his congregation are having their batteries recharged, so that they can let their light shine! He has to be a kind of seer or prophet—not one who just gazes, but one who actually sees. He has to make relationships and connections plain. He has to point a clear path to fortune, to happiness: that is, toward the attitude of believing, trusting and loving which I was describing in the early pages of this book. He must be an activator. Somebody has said: if the world's a stage, the play is for laymen only. The ordained man's role in it is that of prompter. He has to make sure the play does not grind to a halt. He has to be a figure in the background, inspiring confidence. And so you can regard the pulpit, if you like, as the prompter's box. He has to provide room for people to grow. He has to offer a perspective, a way forward. Think of the way Jesus did this for the woman taken in adultery, as I mentioned earlier in this book.

But that is not all. Now that the church is so very outward-looking, the clergyman must not confine his attention to what I would call the private sector of life: the area concerned with marriage, family, children, neighbourhood or district. Since the industrial revolution, the surroundings in which people live and those in which they work have become quite separate. Yet the clergyman has occupied himself almost exclusively with this private sector. And this leads to imbalance. The snag is that the priest may perhaps be able to resolve the tensions in people's private lives (for instance, in the marital sphere), but he has no chance of eliminating the source of all these tensions (for example, the bad structure of the business or industry where the husband works). This is why the clergy are bound to attend to the issues which are central to society and foster a sense of responsibility regarding these questions.

Even in his ordinary contacts with the faithful this changed outlook continues to operate. Now that the church is no longer an end in itself but points away from itself to the world, the priest is often uncertain in his personal contacts. He is neither able nor willing to go on presenting himself directly as the man of a church that imposes obligations and demands on people. One of the main reasons for parish visiting used to be to investigate whether the faithful had been performing their religious duties. In those days 'I do my duty' meant 'I am a good Catholic'. As a pastor he will now have to use a different line of approach. His point of departure will be not the church but the person opposite him. He will have to start from that person's questions; and first and foremost he must be able to listen. He is no longer required to be the man with the answers. He only has to know how to follow the road that must be taken. He must help with the searching. And to bring that off, again and again, is a demanding business. The priest has not really been trained for all this. His whole training has been calculated to teach him how to function inside the church in the very way that we are now abandoning. Thus tremendous emphasis was placed in his studies on, for instance, sacramental doctrine, marital law and morality.

You might sum up the whole change by saying that his authority has shifted from his outfit to his person. In that process a quite different hierarchy emerges : the man who has something to say and inspires confidence is the one who has authority.

The priest–layman relationship

Since the word hierarchy has been uttered, I must say a little more about it. As we saw when we were thinking about the church, a greater emphasis is now being given to the mandate and responsibility laid upon the people of God as a whole. No longer is the mandate restricted to the ordained ministry, or to the bishops.

The days when the word 'church' automatically called to mind pope and bishops are gone. Yet the church is still invariably referred to in the thid person : 'the church must do this or that'. When we talk like that, we are talking about ourselves, in fact, and saying what we ourselves must do. And this restores the priestly office to its true proportions. In the course of history too much emphasis came to be placed upon the ordained ministry; and so the church developed into a body that was top-heavy, but weak-limbed.

It is interesting in this connection to examine where the words 'priest' and 'layman' have really come from. Many religions have priests. A priest is somebody who in a very special way mediates between the deity and the people. He offers sacrifices on behalf of the people to the godhead; and on the god's behalf he blesses the people and dispenses salvation. He acts as intermediary in the contact. It is via him that everything happens. In the New Testament the ordained minister is never called a 'priest' in that sense of the word; nor did Jesus himself exercise his ministry in that way. Jesus did not belong to a priestly family. He even had harsh things to say about the priests of his time : take the parable of the Good Samaritan, for example. All that we can say is this: Jesus' devotion to his Father and to people—a surrender 'even unto death'—made a profound impression. That made it possible for the first Christians to interpret the death of Jesus symbolically as a sacrifice. Jesus was high priest and sacrifice simultaneously. We find this concert worked out in the Letter to the Hebrews. The author's aim was to inform us that through Jesus' definitive and unrepeatable sacrifice the task of the human priesthood had been completely fulfilled and thereby superseded.

In the New Testament therefore any priesthood that is set in opposition to a non-priestly people has ceased to exist. Through Jesus the whole people have become priestly. Through him we have direct access to the Father. Through Jesus we are to offer spiritual sacrifices : not extraneous sacrifices but the offering of ourselves (Hebrews 13:15). Only in that sense may we continue to use the term 'sacrifice' : making a gift of ourselves, surrendering ourselves to people and to God.

Thus Jesus never called himself a priest in the sense we have described; nor for that matter did his disciples. When the Christian movement began to spread to a number of different places, it became necessary for there to be someone in each locality to lead the group of Christians, maintain unity and ensure that the work of Jesus was carried forward in that place. A leader of this kind was designated 'presbyter', meaning 'an elder', 'a leader'. From this word comes our word 'priest'.

What strikes one is that into the term 'presbyter', 'priest', there crept back this meaning of somebody who offers sacrifices, somebody whose task it is to construct a bridge, *in a ritual way*, between God and people. One reason for this development was that in the year 380, under Theodosius, Christianity came to be the religion of the state, so that it officially took the place of the pagan religion of the Romans.

From that moment on, the leaders of the Christian communities began to come to the fore. Everything which until then had obtained in regard to the priests of the Roman religion was transferred to them; and so this idea of ritual mediation between God and man began to come back into favour. The tendency grew and persisted. In that way there gradually re-emerged the kind of priesthood that Jesus had put out of court. We find the traces of this in our old catechism where it is dealing with the eucharist: the Holy Sacrifice of the Mass is identical with Christ's sacrifice on the cross, but celebrated 'in an unbloody way' by means of the priest. As a result of this development the eucharist comes to be seen less and less as the common meal of the whole priestly people of God, and more and more as a sacrifice offered by the priest for and on behalf of the community.

Priests developed into a separate order or class. They were people who knew how to read and write and were therefore held in high esteem. Thus it came about that this one class in the end attracted to itself all kinds of things which were really the concern and right of every believer. The same course of events brought into prominence the word 'layman'—a term which many people in the church today quite rightly feel to be a type of discrimination. Literally, of course, 'layman' means a member of the people (*laïcus*); so you might say that every member of the people of God is both 'layman' and 'priest'—understanding the latter word as it is used in the Letter to the Hebrews.

A similar development has occurred in the case of the word spiritual. Every one of the people of God is 'spiritual', filled with the spirit. In the passage of the centuries this appellation too has become the preserve of a particular group: namely, the 'spiritual' or 'religious' orders, the clerics. To sum up, you might put it like this: everyone is a 'priest', everyone is a 'layman', everyone is 'spiritual'. But within each group of Christians somebody is appointed who goes by the name of presbyter or leader.

Equipping the local congregation

The clergyman must prepare the congregation he is faced with in such a way that they are able to carry out their task. You could formulate the minister's job-description roughly in these terms. As I said before: he is to inspire, stimulate, explain, encourage. His job is principally groundwork, behind the scenes. He must make sure that instead of dozing off, the local church remains on the alert. If the church intends to go on being mobile and adequately prepared, then four things have to be done.

1.   The clergyman must see to it that *liturgy and preaching are well done.* He must be able to express in words what makes this group tick, and unfold what it is that God's word contains for this congregation. I have especially in mind the large, very mixed groups that still turn up at church on Sundays. Many priests find it a worrying business to lead them in worship and to give a sermon. Very often too little actually *happens* at these gatherings. That is because of a certain weakness on the part of the priest, a lack of atmosphere, not enough involvement in the main issues confronting society. Again, the varied motives that bring people to church are one reason why so many of our meetings fail to satisfy. Fortunately, a sifting and sorting process is under way here. More and more people are coming to church to have a little light shed upon their lives and for some vision, some inspiration.

2.   In view of this whole trend it seems likely that the clergy will in future operate more and more *in small-scale situations:* by guiding and inspiring small groups of committed believers, Christians who come together on the basis of a shared type of responsibility or interest in the same questions. Not perhaps with any fixed regularity, but from time to time, according to circumstances. Thus being the church becomes a fact. Such groups may

be very diverse. A number of them already exist: discussion groups, for example, or groups very much concerned with liturgy or with house-visiting. There are groups that concentrate on a critical approach to social issues. Speaking generally we could say that the ordained man who is really to mean something here will have to be someone who has himself been inspired, who has a certain expertise in handling groups and can command confidence.

3. *Individual contacts* too will continue to form an important part of the business of preparing and equipping the local congregation. Personal conversations will mostly be a matter of supplying a direction, a perspective on personal issues; a matter of giving a broader insight into life, of freeing the individual into some possibility of personal fulfilment. What does God's word signify for me, in this situation? Considerable skill is needed here, a skill which partly consists in a capacity to listen hard. The clergyman must not be a man who knows everything.

4. Lastly, there will have to be *catechesis*, instruction and guidance in matters of belief. These days it is no longer just a question of catechizing the children. It is becoming increasingly urgent for a sound catechesis to be provided for adults as well. In our society nobody can afford to rest content with what he was once taught. If a person nowadays wants to remain flexible, if he wants to be 'with it', then he is condemned, as it were, to be the eternal student. And that also applies, naturally enough, in the whole field of religion. The fact is that catechesis nowadays means something very different from what it used to mean. No longer is it just a matter of getting across a number of 'religious truths', but above all of imparting a certain attitude or approach to things. In this connection I have already mentioned religious education at the end of our second chapter.

It becomes increasingly obvious that these four functions cannot any longer be carried out by one person alone; for each of them calls for a lot of expert knowledge and skill. Thus liturgy requires that you be good at reading aloud in public, that you know how to use language well, that you have a certain degree of creativity. For looking after a group you need to have a feeling for what makes the group alive, you have to be able to give a lead and help a group further on its way. For individual conversation you must be able to listen and grow with the other person toward a solution. A catechist must know something of the current vital needs, of the way in which information can be conveyed and assimilated.

Because of these requirements the 'priest of all trades' is getting scarcer. The centipede is a dying species. The clergy are beginning to specialize in one particular line. Catechetics, for instance, has become very much a distinct activity, a full-time job in which some clergy engage. There are also a good many lay people engaged in the teaching of religion at present. Indeed, the running of groups and individual pastoral counselling are activities with which lay people are becoming more and more involved. We refer to lay people trained for the purpose, usually pastoral workers. Even in the liturgy the laity are now active, although the actual conduct of the eucharist is still always reserved to the clergy. Yet this development does raise a number of questions. Who should be ordained nowadays? The catechetist? The pastoral worker? Or just the specialist in liturgy? Is the liturgical function the primary priestly one? Or does it tie up with the development of the 'presbyter' (the leader of the local congregation, with responsibility for everything that happened) into the 'priest' (in the sense of 'sacrificer', 'sacrificial agent')?

Another question is this: what does ordination signify, now that the priest is more harmoniously integrated within the whole people of God?

Who can be an official minister?

After all that, I would just like to mention a few factors which have to be present if somebody wants to qualify as an official minister in the church.

1. *Charisma.* This word means 'grace', 'gift', 'favour'. The minister must have real empathy. He must have a religious commitment. He must be inspired. He must have a feeling for it.

2. *Expertise.* This 'having a feeling for it' must be supported by expert knowledge and skill. I have spoken about this expertise

already. It really is necessary. Generally speaking, good intentions will not in themselves get us very far. On the other hand beneath the professional skill there must also be a touch of inspiration. Otherwise it becomes a matter of acquired techniques from which all the warmth has vanished.

Even so, charisma and professional skill are not yet qualification enough. A lot of lay people have a charisma, are highly expert in one field or another. To qualify for office in the church more is required.

3. *Acknowledgment and acceptance by a local community.* Up to now this point has not been so very much considered in the Catholic Church. We are still at the beginning where this is concerned. What has happened, of course, is that if a priest nominated by the bishop was not welcome, an attempt was very soon made to get the man in question removed. At the moment this provision is beginning to be organized, entirely in keeping with the new image of the church. With this in view the bishops are concerned to build it into their method of appointing. This would mean that those candidates are considered whom the local congregation need because they have charisma and because they have acquired a definite expertise in the area for which there is a need.

4. *Induction or ordination by the bishop.* Acceptance by the local congregation must then be ratified by the bishop. By this gesture the bishop shows his confidence that this minister will do in this particular congregation what the Lord wishes to see done. Through the act of induction this minister is linked up with those in other congregations. Through his ministry the link with the other congregations and with the past is to be preserved. Through his ministry, too, the congregation is to be preserved from disorder.

Acceptance by the congregation and ratification by the bishop are precisely what distinguishes priest from layman. Just these two elements constitute ordination. A lay person may have expertise and charisma, may even be accepted by a particular congregation. But without ratification by the bishop nobody can function as an official minister within a church of which the bishop is the visible sign and token. All four elements are requisite. If somebody has no charisma, for example, has lost the 'feel' of the thing, he will do people more harm than good.

In discussing these four points I have not raised the question as to whether the ordained person should be man or woman, married or single, commissioned for the whole, or only for a part, of his life, doing a full-time job or a part-time extra one. Those issues are not in themselves crucial for deciding whether or not this or that person can function as an ordained minister in the church.

8 Baptism

A few historical notes

Baptism, as you will know, is not something uniquely Christian. Many religions have some sort of baptism, probably because of its very nature water suggests the idea of life and death. Water says something about the mystery of our existence. Water is one of the basic elements that man cannot do without, but which at the same time constitutes a threat for him. That is why from the very earliest times water has played a role in religions, because it has carried this dual meaning of life and death. The individual is immersed: that is to say, the 'old being' dies, is buried, perishes. The man then rises out of the water: that is to say, he is reborn, attains to new life. By virtue of this twofold meaning immersion marks the transition from the one phase to the other.

That was also the significance ascribed by John the Baptist to baptism. He saw that many of his compatriots had lost their way and that religion and life had parted company. So he preached a baptism of repentance. The issue for him was one of total conversion, an about-turn in the direction of the Kingdom of God. Through his words many Jews repented and wanted to turn their back on their life as it had been up to that moment. They wanted to start all over again. And in token of that he immersed people in the Jordan.

Jesus, too, had himself baptized by John. The event began a new phase in his life, devoted entirely to the service of God's kingdom. It was really from that moment that he formally took up his life's work. Just after Easter, Jesus' disciples began to baptize all those who wanted to join their group and make a new start. They baptized in Jesus' name. The name signifies the person. Whoever is baptized in his name belongs to him, has contact with him, breathes his spirit. Such a person wishes to live in the same spirit as Jesus. In his letter to the Christians at Rome, Paul expresses this mystery as follows: 'You have been taught that when we were baptized in Christ Jesus we were baptized in his death; in other words, when we were baptized we went into the tomb with him and joined him in death, so that as Christ was raised from the dead by the Father's glory, we too might live in a new life' (Romans 6:3 and 4).

In the course of the centuries this meaning of baptism was whittled down. There are various reasons why. One has undoubtedly been that baptism came more and more to mean infant baptism. At the same time there was a particular development in the way the church apprehended and expressed its being. The idea that 'outside the church there is no salvation' began to loom increasingly large. You had to be baptized if you were to be saved; for it was baptism that washed away original sin. (May I in this connection say what a pity it is that the act of total immersion has been ousted by that of washing with water. Both are meaningful.) But as I was saying: the act of total immersion marks very clearly the new beginning that is being made. The act of sprinkling has contributed to the distorted notion of original sin as a kind of stain which baptismal water washes away. (Fortunately, there are a few churches which have maintained the act of immersion to this very day, even though it is not very practicable.) This development helped to take the force out of baptism. It became increasingly a sign of adoption into a certain group, and less and less a token of real conversion, of repentance. Almost the opposite. The administering of baptism had certain automatic consequences. Through baptism original sin was remitted. Through baptism heaven was opened for the individual human being. That is why any risk had to be excluded. The infant had to be baptized as soon as possible. Otherwise it might die first! Understandably, this outlook often went with a very skimpy christening ceremony. A handful of people in an empty church. So long as the child was 'done'. Sometimes it even happened that a child was baptized just at the insistence of one of the grandparents. Graham Greene in one of his books has an older woman baptize a child, surreptitiously, on the beach.

74

There is not much chance that that child would get a Christian upbringing, in keeping with its baptism. Yet the woman mutters something to the effect that the baptism is bound to take : like vaccination. Baptism, in this kind of outlook, is seen as 'self-operative', 'automatic'. But this element of automatism is just what we are trying to get away from these days.

A new language for abiding values

We find traces of this approach to things in our old catechisms, which mention three consequences of baptism. These are put into a kind of language that we no longer employ. If we are to take seriously the underlying realities being referred to, we must try and translate these three results of baptism into contemporary terms. It would be naïve on our part simply to dismiss the precious store of values which tradition passes on to us. But it is not easy to reproduce or interpret these values in the language of today. The old catechisms, broadly speaking, present us with three kinds of effect that flow from baptism :

1. it remits original sin,
2. it bestows salvation, and confers a 'mark' on the soul,
3. it makes us members of the church.

These three things don't happen one after the other : they all go together. There is nothing in these three items that is not real, that we cannot subscribe to, but we must translate them into our own terms, and express them in a language that we can understand. I would like to try to do that.

1. What do we mean by 'original sin'? This term is self-contradictory. If a thing is 'original', 'from the origin', then it is something that happened before you existed. But 'sin' implies personal responsibility and personal guilt. Then how are we to understand this term? There can be no doubt that there is a mystery of evil that permeates the world. *A New Catechism* describes original sin as a strange mixture of impotence and guilt. It uses expressions like 'our selfish incapacity to love one another', 'a universal . . . yet inexcusable incapacity to love'. We should not look to the distant past for the sin of Adam. We must look for it in ourselves. Original sin is a kind of sinful situation within mankind,

which each individual human being reinforces and increases by his own personal faults. Original sin is a kind of sinful situation into which each human being is born. You might compare it to a huge snowball that is trundled on from one generation to another, and that grows larger and more threatening all the time. Anyone who sins contaminates others by his sin. He hurts not only his own well-being and happiness but that of others as well. (Look up, in *A New Catechism*, the paragraphs quoted from Anna Blaman, and from John Henry Newman, on pp. 260–261).

2.   And that brings us to the second consequence of baptism: 'salvation'. What does that mean? Again and again throughout the course of history we come across people who want to arrest the snowball of evil and melt it by the very warmth they generate. In this succession of human beings Jesus constitutes for us a high point that has no precedent. His whole life is marked by his assault on the mystery of evil. 'Look, there is the lamb of God that takes away the sin of the world' (John 1:29). Jesus is the living pledge that good will ultimately triumph over evil. He assumed this function quite explicitly at his baptism in the Jordan. He saw his life's work in the sayings uttered by Isaiah about the Servant of Yahweh. This Servant was called to bring about the new future in store for mankind, peace, *shalom*. I have mentioned this before. Now it is into this Jesus that we are baptized; into the sort of life that he led. We are linked up with him. We are grafted on to him. From him comes our inspiration, our perspective on living, our vision of life. Thus we position ourselves within this hopeful movement, where peace, love and reconciliation prevail; where good triumphs over evil and life over death. That is how I would interpret the doctrine that in baptism 'original sin' is remitted. It is not that anything is washed away. Baptism is not something automatic. But there is given to us the possibility, the opportunity to live. An opportunity which also enshrines a mission, a task that bears upon our whole way of life.

3.   And here we find ourselves already engaged with point three : we become members of the church. The community centred in Jesus we refer to as 'church'. Supremely in Jesus Christ the sinful situation which human beings carry with them

is broken through. Anyone who has himself baptized as a ratification of his repentance and conversion, of his being cleansed of his sins, must by the same token overcome the root of every variety of sinfulness in his life: self-seeking and isolation from others. In this way all who have been baptized in Christ are firmly linked together. The death of the 'old man' must be verified, as it were, in a practical kind of solidarity. As with Jesus so with us, baptism should entail a solidarity with the poor and downtrodden in our society. The first Christians went to very considerable lengths in order to demonstrate this (Acts 2:42). We belong, therefore, following in the footsteps of Jesus, to the group bent on working to bring into existence a better and more humane world. Thus the whole point of baptism is the realization of a worldwide brotherhood. Whenever we recall our baptism, we should be inspired to that end.

Infant baptism

So far we have been talking about baptism, in general, and not about infant baptism. Yet it is the baptism of infants that usually concerns people. This is a controversial area at the moment. There is one thing I would like to make clear at once: the single term 'baptism' is used for two quite different things: infant baptism and the baptism of adults. If we can be clear about this, then we have at least a foot to stand on in the uncertain questions centred on infant baptism today. To fail to distinguish the two leads to muddled thinking, and to pointless arguments. For example, Karl Barth, the great Protestant theologian, fiercely opposed infant baptism, right to the end of his life; so do many other people. To them, baptism must involve an element of believing, of choosing, and a baby cannot do these things.

You meet parents today who say, 'I'm not forcing my child to accept one particular way of life; I don't want to label him from infancy; he may reject it all later; he must choose for himself when he's old enough, I'm not going to make a choice for him.' This sort of remark also confuses the issue between infant and adult baptism. This is not surprising, when we consider how little the practice of the church has helped in making the distinction. In the past, the form of infant baptism was little more than a shortened version of adult baptism. People certainly thought that at the moment of the administration of baptism, something was bound to happen, even with a child. Remember the consequences of baptism we listed from the old catechisms (p. 75).

But, I can hear you asking, do I mean that nothing does happen at infant baptism? Properly performed, a great deal happens. But nothing is added which was not there before. The baptism provides nothing new which as it were descends upon the child from on high. That is why the phraseology we used to employ to denote the consequences of baptism is so misleading. What really goes on, then, when a child is baptized? God is constantly occupied with us human beings. He operates through people. We are permitted to cooperate in God's creation. When parents produce a child, they are cooperating in God's creation in a unique way. If God has made a start with something, he does not drop it; which is also why this child has been born not for death but for life. For Christians, death is not the end. Of course the child will die, just as Jesus too died. Hence it is dipped in the font. It will 'go under'. But that is not the end of it. It will live, as Jesus lives. That is why it is raised up again, out of the water. I said before what a pity it is that in the majority of churches the act of immersion has been replaced by an act of washing. Nothing is cleansed or washed away; but it is visibly demonstrated that this child has no need to sink down into evil and death.

That parents may play their part in God's creation, that their child is born for life and not for death—this is what they wish gratefully to express and affirm and capture in that moment of baptism, in order the better to retain it, to ensure its continuance and handle the consequences it entails for the child's upbringing. On the basis of their child's baptism the parents are encouraged to bring it up in a Christian way. This line of approach puts the emphasis very much on the parents and also, although to a lesser extent, on the godparents, those who represent that big group outside the family which will also have its share in bringing up the child. You might say that the parents are baptized 'in association with' their child. That comes out clearly in the wording of the new baptismal rite. It is the parents who are addressed, rather than the child. In infant baptism we are made to see what these days of delight and joy are really all about.

You occasionally hear parents say: surely we can bring our

children up as Christians without getting them baptized? Of course you can. But baptism is meant to provide a stimulus to that upbringing. As parents, you have to get the strength you need from somewhere. So, in the new baptismal rite, the questions that were first put to you during the marriage rite are asked of you again. 'Will you accept children lovingly from God, and bring them up according to the law of Christ and his Church?' When a child is born, these questions become live issues again. So there is no conflict between having the child baptized and all that parents do otherwise in the interests of their child. Everything that parents do for their child influences that child. If infant baptism is not just an empty gesture to the parents, it will not fail to have its effect on the child.

You also get parents who do indeed want to have their child baptized but who have no firm connection with the church. Still, some sort of link with the church is necessary, in one form or another, otherwise the baptism remains an isolated gesture. Parents have to take their bearings on Jesus Christ, so to speak, and continually redirect their lives to him. Then you have parents—often in the case of mixed marriages—who do not want their child baptized into a particular church but into *the* church of Jesus Christ. This is fine in principle, but still difficult to achieve in practice; for *the* church of Christ is there in a number of different churches. Happily, in our day they are moving closer and closer to one another all the time. For the child itself baptism need have no legally binding consequences. Later in life he will have to decide for himself whether he wants to go on in the way he was brought up, or not. That is why today, when we find ourselves caught up in the transition from a 'tribal church' to one that we belong to by deliberate choice, we are searching to discover the moment when a youngster is able to make such a choice. Is it when he or she leaves junior school? Probably not. Again, the age of 18 does not seem ideal. And what form should the choice take? Might confirmation be the right moment? What is the actual relationship between confirmation and adult baptism?

9 The breaking of bread

There are, as you know, innumerable questions currently being raised about the eucharist. Diverse questions. Why is church attendance dwindling so rapidly? Why has the eucharist suddenly ceased to draw people? Or has that been going on for much longer than we think? How should the eucharist be celebrated, if there is to be a link with ordinary, everyday life?

A kind of discontent is abroad. The changes already made in the way the eucharist is conducted, generally speaking, go only a modest way toward meeting the expectations people have. And those expectations vary a great deal—so much so, in fact, that some priests are reduced almost to despair. For one group of church members find all these modifications simply enervating: a watering down of everything they used to experience in the Mass. Others again, however, find the eucharist still too far divorced from their ordinary life. They get far too little inspiration from it; it does not supply their need. And a lot of people in both groups are staying away.

You do not get rid of these difficulties by continually tinkering with the form of the eucharistic services. Of course, a more intelligible kind of language, more easily comprehended gestures, a greater degree of clarity and so on are all necessary. But the problems that surface in this area have very deep roots. They are bound up with the whole process of renewal in the world and in the church. The changes are naturally felt most of all in those channels of expression in which, ever since our younger days, we have invested much of our religious life and experience: confession and eucharist, the sacraments we received most frequently.

80

The eucharist contains many possible varieties of experience

'. . . in each period of church history new facets and values are revealed in this so divinely simple gesture. At one time Christians stress their unity. At other times, thanksgiving to the Father. Then again, the sacrifice. Or Jesus' presence. And there must still be treasures as yet undiscovered within the mystery. Jesus is always new in his greatest mystery.

'The church has been charged to transmit and safeguard this gift. It is convinced that the Spirit of God will not permit it to err in this matter. Hence in the course of centuries, councils of the church have pronounced upon it. They did not aim at determining exhaustively and for all time all the truth of the mystery. The words they used were often formulations meant to defend very definite Christian truths and values at a certain period, against certain errors. To understand properly the teachings of the councils, one must always ask : what Christian and evangelical values were at stake at the time? When we know what was being defended, we must then proclaim the same truths in the language of our own day' (*A New Catechism*, p. 334).

Official statements are the sort of pronouncements which you have to read carefully several times before you can even begin to appreciate the consequences that flow from them. We have just emerged from a period when our religious knowledge and conduct and experience reflected an attitude that can be summed up as: everything is fixed; it will always be like this; it's unalterable. Under the influence of a quite new and open atmosphere we are beginning to become very much aware that what we were taught (the spirit of the old catechism) was no more than a momentary flash, a mere 'snap' in the history of Christianity as a whole: one very much determined by a post-Tridentine theology strongly biased against the Reformers. A type of doctrine and religious practice which, particularly when it came to the eucharist, put the main stress on certain values that were in danger of being swamped by the Reformation. That was very right and proper. But such an emphasis was of course somewhat one-sided; and that one-sidedness is at last beginning to be felt now, when quite different ways of apprehending the eucharist are emerging as real possibilities, possibilities inherent in the eucharist itself.

'The deeper a symbol is rooted in the realities of everyday life —eating and drinking, body and blood—the greater the multiplicity of meanings that it contains' (*A New Catechism*, p. 341). This is precisely what a lot of people find so problematical at the moment. 'It was all made so clear to us and was such a devotional experience!'

Well, yes. But it is also a fact that for many people the old way of thinking about the eucharist and responding to it no longer offers any real inspiration for living the Christian life today.

We also see today the piety and spirit of devotion that grew up around the eucharist draining away. To mention a few: Benediction, the forty-hour prayer, exposition of the Blessed Sacrament, processions with the Blessed Sacrament, eucharistic fasting, and so on. These are all manifestations which fitted a period during which the *presence of Jesus* in the eucharist was given tremendous emphasis. A mode of experience in which the consecration and transubstantiation had a major place; for the whole thing, at a personal level, was centred around the sacred host.

The Lord is indeed present where people celebrate the eucharist together. But whereas this presence was seen originally in the action as a whole (doing what Jesus did during the last supper), it later came to be narrowed down to one point, to one moment (the moment of consecration when Jesus came down upon the altar). The primary emphasis here was something like this: the Lord gives himself to you; the Lord comes into you; Jesus comes into your heart; Jesus is food for your soul. A highly meditative, introverted piety. And so a lot of time was set aside for meditation and adoration, for every possible sort of religious exercise. And every now and then this devotion would express itself in monumental acts of homage. The eucharistic congresses are examples of this. Enjoying a dash of real Roman excitement and pious enthusiasm.

In our own day a quite different sort of devotion has sprung up: one that is in step with a much more outward-directed, outward-looking sense of what it is to be the church. A more extrovert zeal. A consciousness that does not bestow all that amount of time on personal adoration and meditation.

There is a very different turn of mind nowadays. People want to think and reflect together and if possible to reach a common course of action on that basis. It is a mode of experience less centred on the person of Jesus (only think of the 'bridal mystique' which for a long time has been the main experience of so many nuns and was a typical feature of all eucharistic piety). Now much more attention is paid to the Jesus who is prepared to stick up for the underdog. Perhaps I may just be allowed to quote in this connection this statement:

'In the spirituality of today the pull is exercised not so much by Christ's person as by his teaching of love, justice and peace. For many people Christ has become more the One sent to proclaim the world's salvation than the Man of Sorrows with whom life is to be shared through an intimate participation. Nowadays he points away from himself to the world and its sufferings. So for many a Christian his relationship to the Lord as a believer is felt more as a command to go out into the world in the spirit of Jesus than as a way of fleeing out of the world to him for refuge' (Report 4, third plenary session of the Dutch Pastoral Council, 'The Christian's moral attitude to life in the world', pp. 13–14).

What this statement is really saying is that the best way to keep a person's memory alive is to make his ideals come true. There is nothing permanent or timeless about our particular way of apprehending the eucharist. We are aware of that. Within our generation a shift of values is taking place in every conceivable sphere; and that has made us cautious of saying anything is 'for ever'. Our whole religious awareness—and this includes our encounter with the eucharist—is obviously coloured by the world we live in. The eucharist always remains the source from which all these trends and currents are able to arise; so we have to be extremely careful before we say something is a 'superficializing', an 'adaptation', a 'watering-down', of the eucharistic event. Newly apprehended values evoke new terms, a new language of gestures, a new form.

We can distinguish three ways in which people have talked about the eucharist: chronologically, these have followed one after the other, at different periods of time. But now they co-exist

—and this sometimes gives rise to confusion. These three variations—each of which has had great influence—are:

1. The priest offers the holy sacrifice of the Mass.
2. We celebrate the eucharist.
3. We come together to break bread with and for one another.

In discussions on the new approach, old terms are frequently employed—which is rather confusing.

It is difficult, too, to be prepared to discover some particular aspect of 'Holy Mass' in 'the breaking of bread'. Sometimes one does not know whether one should speak of 'sacred host', 'bread' or 'holy bread'. For some the use of the word 'bread' is a frontal attack on the mystery of the eucharist—another example of identifying the eucharist with an instant in its history. Understandable, of course, but still pretty stifling: in the scriptural account of its institution we read that Jesus took bread. Nothing more and nothing less.

Is there really such a gap between those who use the older expression, and talk about Holy Mass, and those who talk about the breaking of bread? Really, we have already dealt with this question when we were talking about the more introverted type of piety and the more outward-directed spirituality. They are two sides of the coin we call the eucharist—but they derive from very different periods of history. Between the two, in historical terms, came the phrase 'celebrating the eucharist' (remember that eucharist means thanksgiving). A few years ago there was a lot of emphasis on this 'thanksgiving' aspect of the Mass: giving thanks to the Father for all creation, for the life we can live in Jesus Christ. This is certainly a basic part of the Mass; but yet, at the present moment, it does not hold quite the central position that it did a little while ago.

The attitude we express in the phrase 'celebrating the eucharist' does not lay such one-sided emphasis on the presence of Jesus as the attitude expressed by the 'holy sacrifice of the Mass' does. So the words of consecration, instead of being the high, focal point of the whole Mass, were seen to fit more harmoniously into the whole action of the celebration of the eucharist. And after the Vatican Council, the ringing of bells at this point began to be less dominant. The celebration again became the action of the entire community, and not simply of the priest.

Given that the centre of gravity shifted from the words of consecration to the celebration as a whole, what is now happening, with the emphasis described in our phrase 'coming together in the breaking of bread', is to turn the whole event in an outward direction, away from ourselves. And though we may no longer use the word 'sacrifice' to describe the action, this is absolutely what the word 'sacrifice' meant.

Before we go any further, I would like to express what I have said with a diagram, and a table.

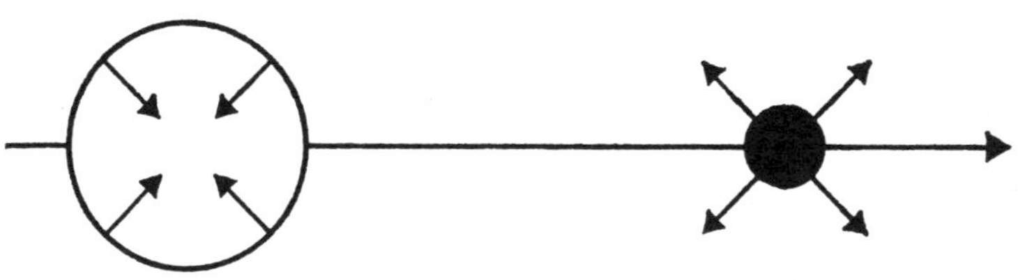

The priest offers the sacrifice of the Mass	We celebrate the eucharist	We come together to break bread with and for one another
Presence of the Lord	Giving thanks to the Father	
Consecration	1. Action of the whole community	
Transubstantiation	2. The consecration harmoniously taken up into the whole	
Self-centred spirituality		Extroverted spirituality
Benediction, 40-hour prayer, Procession of the Blessed Sacrament		

The breaking of bread

For the Jews, before the meal began, bread was broken and blessed; and the meal came to an end with the blessing of the cup. Between these two actions, the meal was eaten; they framed the meal and symbolized it. The term 'breaking of bread' came to mean the whole meal. From this setting the eucharist has emerged. Originally it formed the framework of a meal shared together by a group of people. Very early on, both actions (with the bread and the cup) were moved to the close of the meal. Then finally the meal as such completely disappeared, because the symbolic gesture of breaking the bread often contrasted very sharply indeed with what was actually going on at the table (consider the quite unambiguous remarks made by Paul in I Corinthians 11).

In the earliest texts we find a persistent use of the term 'the breaking of bread' (Acts 2:42–46; Acts 20:7; Luke 24:13 ff.). If we read the stories concerning the miraculous multiplication of the loaves, it would seem to be inexhaustible as an event. The important point is that during this earliest period eucharist and communal meal were closely bound up together. Only gradually did they grow apart because the intention behind the breaking of bread was no longer properly understood. When the common meal fell into disuse the eucharist was celebrated on its own. This separation has obviously given rise to a kind of estrangement between the eucharist and the big, communal meals which people hold from time to time, and because of that also an alienation from the ordinary, everyday business of eating. This connects up, perhaps, with the distinction between sacred and profane.

On the basis of this historical evidence, I would like to offer the following proposition : the eucharist affords a dimension that can act as a foundation for all our communal meals. Of course, this needs some more thinking about. But at any rate we must not do anything that, for a child, will foster the gap between the two. When is a child ready for the eucharist? We should not seek to grapple with this question so much along the lines of 'when the child can tell the difference between the bread of the eucharist and ordinary bread', but much more in terms of 'when the child begins to perceive the deeper values to be experienced in the act of eating together' (the breaking of the bread with and for one another). This is the direction in which the eucharistic training of the child should move; and then the eucharist will not become excessively ritualized nor too much divorced from ordinary life. It will then retain its symbolic power, its power to mean something in ordinary life. This symbolic power, after all, is what the eucharist should possess as a sacrament.

The eucharist as sacrament

Three times *A New Catechism* uses the phrase 'prophetic action' in speaking of the last supper. In a simple, familiar gesture, Jesus represents his self-offering, his self-offering 'even unto death'. In this action he gives himself. It is the expression, in a single action, of his whole life, up to and including his death. It is an intense moment, a moment of concentrated experience. A moment at which, in a single action and in a simple utterance, much sweat and effort, commitment and struggle become suddenly and clearly illuminated. It could hardly be clearer. A prophetic action. You can find this kind of gesture in various places in the Old Testament, too, and especially in the prophet Jeremiah. To give just two examples. In Jeremiah 19:10, the prophet smashes a jug to pieces, to show the people the Lord's warning of what will happen to them if they do not alter their behaviour. The same point is made in the splendid image of the yoke of Babylon (Jeremiah 27). A prophetic action, therefore, that has a definite bearing on the sacramental character of the eucharist.

In the eucharist, on Christ's own instruction, we break bread with and for one another with the purpose of realizing the very attitude and demeanour of Jesus Christ in our lives. Again and again we bring this purpose to life within ourselves; and for that reason we believe that, however imperfectly, we too can make it a reality. Thus the sacraments give verbal expression (and indeed more than that) to a fundamental human posture to which Christ has given greater depth. We acknowledge together the 'Christlike' values and on this basis are better able to put them into practice.

So when we celebrate the eucharist we are doing what Jesus did, both on that evening before his passion and throughout his life, up to the point of death: giving oneself for the well-being of others. 'Do this in remembrance of me' refers therefore to his whole attitude to life, not just to an isolated gesture. In *his* life it was furthest of all from being an isolated gesture.

How are we to break bread?

The expression 'the breaking of bread' is becoming a very popular way of referring to the eucharist. As a descriptive phrase it has been spread around by a variety of movements. For example, the group that calls itself 'Shalom'. They are the source of the expression: 'Break [bread] till we are whole'. And in the document they have produced we read, for example: 'Break and share, until everything is whole, in a sacred order, until all of us together—the whole people comprising all peoples, no one excepted—are able to see that it is good.' Here you can see at once how great is the unity that exists between symbolic gesture and life itself.

Another group which has given much prominence to this 'breaking of bread' is the action-group for a vernacular liturgy, in Amsterdam. Huub Oosterhuis especially has expressed this idea in a number of lyrics. Just to give you an example I quote the final stanza of a 'song about this place where we have met together'.

> Table of One, bread for the knowing
> that we are given, each to the other.
> Marvel of Godhead, people at peace,
> old and forgotten, mystery new.
> Breaking and sharing, be the impossible,
> do the unthinkable, dying to rise again.

Here the 'breaking of bread' is clearly the action we perform together. This name for the eucharist, a name which expresses a different approach to our way of experiencing it, has gradually percolated into more general use. Here and there it is made evident by the form of the ritual. Either there is a special breaking of bread by the priest, where the celebrant breaks pieces from a single large loaf for distribution, or people literally break the bread for one another. For a figure like Camillo de Torres too the breaking of bread was of vital relevance. He took it so seriously that he was unable to justify the divorce between it and the harsh reality he saw all around him. It became the reason for his ceasing to exercise the office of a priest. He wrote to his bishop:

'Within the present structure of the church it is impossible for me to continue exercising my outward, cultic priesthood. After all, the Christian's priesthood does not consist solely in the celebration or observance of external rites. The eucharist has a fundamentally communal function: the breaking of the

bread. The Christian community cannot celebrate this, therefore, if it is not effectively sharing its life with its neighbour.'

Although the action of breaking bread is not an obvious element
of our culture, nevertheless it would appear to be meaningful
to a lot of people in our day. It is a primary human gesture
which can apparently transcend differences of culture.

Thus the breaking of bread gives the whole observance an
outward-looking character, focussing as it does upon the com-
mission and the task entrusted to us. Yet even this new evaluation
can become a caricature, if the strong emphasis on our 'mission'
means that the element of inwardness, of interior concentration,
is more or less obliterated—or if the outward-looking posture
entails no more than a vague and romantic errand which gets
nowhere and which leaves everything as it was before. Two
obvious dangers, therefore.

So far as the first is concerned, our eucharistic celebrations
run the risk of becoming tremendously 'activist'. Too matter-of-
fact, making too exclusive an appeal to our sense of the responsi-
bilites that are ours. And if in addition we are still confronted
with tasks too great for us, then the eucharist as sacrament is
swallowed up in a fog. The person who is being sent out must
then leave the call unanswered. He sees himself relapsing into
a kind of impotence. His heart stays closed and cold. Whereas
the very purpose of the sacrament is to encourage, stimulate,
inspire and provide the motive power that will enable us to carry
out what we see to be our mission. That will only be possible if
in the eucharistic celebration we really have encountered something, if something has happened in us and to us. And if this
experience simply never comes, then one can understand such
reactions as : 'Aren't we just sitting here wasting our time? So
what's the point of a celebration like that? People should just
be good, get around to a bit of real involvement, in so far as
they can manage it in the circumstances.' The question we should
really be asking is where in God's name am I going to keep on
getting the strength and the courage for the commitment that is
asked of me? Then we might indeed get at the real meaning of
the sacrament.

As regards the second danger, of romanticism : the instruction
to action has to be clear, the stand to be taken more or less well

defined. It must not get bogged down in vague notions of 'helping to build a better world' or 'being nice to one another'. Such sentiments are too grand and change nothing.

In our celebrations of the eucharist we shall have to grow toward practical ways of caring. Perhaps in the shape of being keen to take up causes, expressions of support, forms of protest. In the spirit of the prayer: give us this day our daily bread, as we also give their daily bread to others. The eucharist must not bear the stamp of a pressure-group.

Nor indeed of an institute for social criticism. Yet our repeatedly reminding ourselves in this way of our Lord's attitude to life will bring us no joy unless this same action can also be carried through into the life of every day.

Now 'everyday life' is something different for each individual. One may be eking out his days in a home for the aged. Another may be a child at junior school. Yet another a teacher or a housewife. One may be full of ideas, another may have very few. One person will have a bent for action, even large-scale action, while another's strong points will lie in his consideration for the people around him. Yet all these relate continually to one and the same thing: breaking (of bread) till we are whole. And that can be realized in every possible key. In the elderly person whom it eventually brings round to listening quietly to someone else, instead of going on and on about himself; in the young activist, making his way to the House with signs and placards.

It is totally wrong to blame people for being a-political, for you must not expect everybody to adopt a clear position. From people who level accusations of that sort we may perhaps require a more productive standpoint than the one they actually adopt. But in all these cases the same thing applies: as a human being we are all easily disappointed, easily prejudiced, quickly found in a particular corner, soon back where we started. So every time we come back to the question: where in God's name do you acquire the wherewithal to find the right approach? We must be continually crossing the threshold. When an individual fulfils the task in front of him, he is answering to God's purpose. When he works for the well-being of others, and hence for his own, he is serving and honouring God. That, in a concentrated and explicit form, is what he comes face to face with in the action of breaking and sharing out and eating the bread.

90

Breaking the bread must be celebrating, too

It is a grand thing when people of every sort and condition come together to celebrate and give thanks for the fact that they are human beings, that they can be human beings. We not only break the bread with and for one another; we also eat of it together. There should be a glint, a flash here and there, of what we read about for instance in Acts 2:42–47: the powerful sense of solidarity, the mutual ties that bound Christians together. They had everything in common. Nobody was allowed to go short of anything. This solidarity was given expression in the common meal.

We celebrate the self-giving of the Lord. By giving his life for others the Lord by the manner of his living nullified in principle the foundation of all man's divisiveness (sin). That has to be expressed. That has to be felt. In principle it is possible to remove every form of isolation from the world. That is why from the earliest times the eucharist has been called *sacramentum unitatis*, the sacrament of unity: the visible sign of the possibility that in Jesus Christ men need no longer treat each other on a wolf-and-lamb basis. 'Be the impossible, do the unthinkable.' That is to celebrate. We often use the word 'celebration'; yet in many cases it is not a genuine celebration. What happens does not warm the heart.

10 The sacramental remission of sins

Some background to the decline in private confessions

The effects of what is happening today are most clearly seen in the sacrament of confession. Within a relatively short period of time, confession has been reduced to a minimum. Various factors have been at work here, factors closely related to the changing patterns of thought and living that prevail today, and to the reorientation of religious practice and belief that have resulted. I will set down a few of these, in a rather arbitrary order:

1. In our generation, all that was at one time taken for granted is exposed to questioning. Ancient customs are being re-examined, and judged on their merits.

2. As soon as the question 'why' is asked about any traditional practice that has gone on for generations, it becomes apparent that the thing is entirely relative. Established practices are conditioned by the time in which they first arose. If you read scripture, and examine the history of the sacrament of penance, you cannot help being struck by the many and various forms that confession has taken down the centuries. It is part of this same historical process that is today throwing up a new form of penitential service alongside private confession.

3. A lot of people have begun to ask themselves what exactly they are doing when they go to confession, and have come to realize that what they have been confessing as sins often had very little to do with what was really happening in their daily lives.

92

4. Bound up with this is the whole shift of emphasis away from a religion of obligation to personal responsibility. When one is keeping the rules laid down by others, there is very little need for a personal stand on the issues; but when the responsibility shifts to the individual, the situation changes. A person steeped from childhood in a duty-ethic ('I am a good Catholic because I fulfil my obligations') must find it hard to accuse himself of sin within a morality that is beginning to take the notion of personal responsibility as its starting-point. He will first have to learn how to recognize where his personal responsibility lies.

5. Furthermore, the changed view of sexual matters has led a lot of people to go to confession less frequently.

6. Speaking generally, one may say that a great deal of anxiety, of scrupulousness, has disappeared, and with it a great deal of the need to go to confession. The direct connection between going to confession and going to communion has gone. Gone, too, is the anxious concern about being in a state of grace, in case the Lord should come like a thief in the night.

7. In a social context, too, the priest's position as the only person people could talk to has been diminished. A lot of taboos have vanished. It is much easier nowadays to talk to people you really trust about very personal matters. And because of the pace of life today, it is much more necessary to do so than it used to be. There are times when a man must have his say, must talk himself out. You still hear it said sometimes: 'Since private confession has been on the decrease the psychiatrists' consulting-rooms have been crowded out.' If the point being made here has to do with a chronological sequence, I accept it—but not if the sequence is supposed to be a causal one.

8. The point of going to confession is no longer clear to many people. If you have settled this or that score with God or with your fellows, then there seems no need to take it to the confessional. And so the baby looks in danger of disappearing with the bath-water. What, if anything, can this sacrament still mean?

Is it actually still possible to commit sin?

Such a remark would sound very strange to someone who has grown up with the old definition of sin as each and every voluntary transgression of the law of God. However, I would like to go into some of the reasons why we have gradually outgrown this old idea of sin.

1.   The definition itself strikes us as too legalistic. It is far too superficial. In most spheres today, we find people have reservations about regulations and a considerable emphasis is placed on personal conscience and responsibility. We do not want to be told what we should do exclusively from on high or from outside. We like to decide for ourselves how to act, in accordance with our own conscience. This does not mean that law as such is done away with or rendered superfluous. But people are looking for new forms of authority. At any rate, we are not so keen nowadays on talking about 'God as lawgiver', or about the 'law of God'. Phrases like these detract too much from our own responsibility, and put the onus too far outside ourselves.

2.   The old definition is facile, because it equates sin with the *exterior, sinful act,* whereas it is far more important to discover the attitude from which our sinful actions arise. When sin is seen as transgression of law, you can register precisely whether somebody has broken the law or not. Thus all kinds of distinctions were made in the past between venial sin and mortal sin. By measuring sin in this way the gravity of sin has to some extent been lost sight of. In the end various 'breaches' of the law which were not sins at all came to be regarded as sin. 'I missed Mass on Sunday.' 'Why?' 'I was ill.' That, we quite rightly feel, shows a false understanding of sin. But it shows how for many people a major cleavage arose between what they confessed as sin and their own world of thinking and living. They would call 'sin' things which did not touch them inwardly, did not pain them, did not keep them awake at night, but which they would confess, 'just to be on the safe side'. I came across a similar train of thought in a little song by Ramses Shaffy: 'Love causes pain, love leaves wounds, but love is a beautiful thing, and it's no sin.' Does love as Shaffy understands it—his song is about the tragedy

94

of divorce—a love which causes pain and leaves wounds, really have nothing to do with sin?

3.   And that lands us plumb in the middle of the next point. The old definition fails to emphasize sufficiently the *destructive effect* sin has *on the person who commits it*. Sin drags the individual concerned down to destruction. Sin isolates him, makes him lonely, estranges him from himself. And it cannot simply be shaken off, discarded like an overcoat, by evasion, by getting away from wherever it was the mischief was done. If a man does not learn to take the hard way back to his humanity, to the fulness of being a human being (repentance), and to keep taking that way, the sin will make him ill and carry him to his destruction. Perhaps we may put it like this: a thing is not bad because you are doing what is prohibited, but it is *prohibited* because it is bad for you. The only reason for the law's existence is in fact to defend and protect human happiness and well-being.

4.   In direct conjunction with the previous point we should say that sin undermines the existence not only of the person involved but of others as well. Sin has a *corrupting effect on the very environment* in which somebody is living. Sin puts all the community in bond. Evil, sin, makes life impossible, taints the atmosphere, warps relationships between people. It generates a coldness from which one can only want to retreat. This social (or rather, a-social) character of sin was not sufficiently apparent in the old definition. We are more conscious than ever nowadays of the many ties that bind us with people all around us. It is totally untrue, therefore, when somebody says: it is up to me whether I think or do this or that, I'm not hurting anybody else. Other people most definitely do feel the consequences of our depressions and headaches.

These four comments prompted by the old notion of sin have brought us very close to a new understanding. The God who gives his orders from on high is making way for the God who calls us in many different kinds of circumstance; which is why it is important for us to learn to understand God's call in the situations in which we find ourselves. For it is in these situations that our task, our mission, is laid out. To the extent that a man discovers and fulfils his proper task he will become whole, he will become a fully fledged human being. Or to put it in the language of the church: the kingdom of God will be his.

Notice how often, these days, the same phrases keep cropping up: for whatever reason, people will not or dare not assume the responsibility which is theirs: 'they wouldn't know', 'they couldn't care less', 'they don't want to get their hands dirty', 'they don't want to get involved', 'you can't be too careful'.

Obviously, all this puts a different emphasis on sin. We have always been taught to regard Adam's sin as a sin of pride. He wanted to be equal with God. He wanted to be more than man, more than human. But the prevailing sin today is different: man wants to be *less* than human. He does not want to know. I pass, he says; you can count me out. The American theologian, Harvey Cox, rightly observes that this aspect is also clearly present in the fall of our first parents. The first thing that Adam and Eve did was to repudiate the task allotted to them in the created world. Instead of mastering creation, of living in harmony with creation as a whole, they asked an animal what they should do. So Cox felt able to confront contemporary man with the injunction contained in the title of one of his books: 'Don't leave it to the snake'. And once Adam and Eve had sinned, they hadn't the nerve to accept responsibility for their action. They shuffled it off, Adam on to Eve, Eve on to the serpent. Much as you might say: 'I dinna ken', or 'orders is orders'.

Not only has the whole notion of sin altered, but also the image of the ideal human being. If pride is the main sin, then the most virtuous individual is the man who is humble, obedient, dutiful and submissive. That has always been our picture of the saints—an ideal which many no longer think either worthy or desirable. For now that not wanting to know, inertia, inactivity is the major sin, a quite different image of the ideal man emerges: he is the man with the nerve to step into the breach, who refuses to turn the blind eye, even though it may cost him his reputation, his job or his life. I need only mention the names of Pope John, Mgr. Bekkers, the Kennedys, Camillo Torres, Martin Luther King. Think how we used to be taught to think of Jesus as one who was obedient, dutiful and meek, whereas now we see him as the man who stuck up for the poor and outcast. That cost *him* his life, too. As a matter of fact, even the saints were different, more often than not, from the picture we were given of them in our younger days.

Thus pride and apathy are set more or less at opposite poles; yet they are not mutually exclusive. They are still two principal sources of a great deal of suffering and misery, even if in one age the accent has been on pride, and in another on indifference.

The remission of sins happens in our ordinary, everyday life

What does forgiving—the remission of sins—mean? Let me put it in very broad perspective. I have defined sin as: not wanting or not venturing to assume or recognize one's responsibility, not wanting to know, to own up; and in that sense Adam willed not to be a man. Forgiveness—the *remission* of sin—I would define in these terms: as opposed to Adam, Jesus did will to be a man. And he was so in the full sense of the word. In him man has resumed his responsibility, has taken it up again. In him, therefore, man is able to keep returning from his wanderings and take up once more his proper task, his mission and his responsibility. That is why Jesus is the fount of all forgiveness. Jesus lives on among his followers. In this fellowship, therefore, in the church, there is forgiveness of sins. Forgiveness is never an automatic thing. Forgiveness is something of great substance and value. Nobody can afford to disregard it. This we know from personal experience. It preys on conscience till the heart grows cold.

To forgive is to accept the other person once more, despite what has happened. To be forgiven is to be accepted back by others—to be accepted on a basis of the possibilities Jesus offers to us. In Jesus man has a future, a 'further on'. Nobody need lose his dynamic, his momentum; and no one need end up alienated from his humanity, his being a human being. There is always a way back. There is always forgiveness. That forgiving is extremely difficult, no one can deny. But it is possible, for everyone, in Jesus.

The major premiss from which we should proceed in this matter is as follows: it is *where we have done amiss* that we have also to acknowledge our guilt, *it is there too that we must ask forgiveness.* In other words, forgiveness takes place in normal, everyday living, and only there. The two questions which this proposition immediately raises are these: *can someone invariably* make amends for his blunder exactly where he committed it? Say, for instance, that in a certain locality you have cast a slur on somebody's reputation. How should you make amends for that? Or through various circumstances you put your foot in it one day and say or do the wrong thing in what is normally a happy marital relationship. Will your wife or husband ever be able to understand that situation? And the second question is this: where it is possible to put things right on the spot, *does it in fact happen that way*? Or do we at times go barging so clumsily through life that we just never notice how much hurt our behaviour is causing to others?

If a negative answer has not infrequently to be given to both questions, then the church as a community is faced here with a twofold task. For as I said: the church's job is to keep forgiveness alive. Where restitution on the spot is quite impossible, the task of the church is so to reconcile the person concerned to what has happened that he is able to go on again. Where making good the damage at once is simply not possible, it is the church's duty to keep in being the need and the longing for forgiveness.

Let us for a moment go more deeply into this argument that forgiveness has to take place in daily life. You may be wondering: does it matter whether a husband asks his wife directly for forgiveness, or has forgiveness for having affronted his wife notified to him in the sacrament? What is the connection between the two? We should not construe these two factors by saying that after he has obtained his wife's forgiveness he must still ask God to forgive him. After all, we have learnt that that is not the way to talk about God. God works through man, not side by side with him. God's call, his appeal, comes to us in and through the situation we find ourselves in. But what then is the connection here?

To find an answer to our question we would do best to turn back to the practice of the early church. From the third to the sixth century the confession and remission of sin took a striking form. Only a few offences were confessed in those days: murder, adultery and idolatry; and they had to be notorious, a matter of public knowledge. The person concerned would acknowledge his *faux pas* before the bishop, in the presence of the entire congregation; and the bishop would then confirm that the individual in question had made himself intolerable as a member of this community. But not permanently. The bishop sent the offender to join the company of penitents. That it to say, he was given a chance to return. But he had first to show that he really meant it; and so he had to carry out some arduous form of penance, which might last for a year or even for several years. When he had done that, he was formally received back into the community by the bishop—an event which usually took place during Holy Week. The bishop then confirmed that this person had made amends and therefore the community accepted him back. If you have followed me so far, you will have noticed three things happening here: the bishop confirms that such and such a member of the group is a sinner, and he makes that clear by a symbolic action: he expels him. Next the bishop declares that even in his case expiation and forgiveness are possible, and he can be readmitted; and that too the bishop demonstrates in a symbolic gesture: he sends the penitent off to the company of penitents. Finally, after the period of penance, the bishop confirms that all is right again, indicating that with yet another gesture: he formally reinstates the penitent within the community. It is the visible evident character that the bishop gives to all this that we refer to as the sacrament.

You will notice here the three components of confession, satisfaction and forgiveness which have always been the basis of the sacraments: *confession*—owning up—*satisfaction*—making amends—and *forgiveness*. Notice the sequence.

From the seventh and eighth centuries onward this distinct form disappeared, thanks to the activities of Irish and Eastern monks. The community aspect sank more and more into the background. People took to confessing all sorts of minor sins. This was done in private, two persons only being present, without the community having any clearly marked role in the matter. In that way the whole thing took on quite a different character; so that eventually, in the sixteenth century, there emerged what we now describe as the confessional. Especially when people started to put a great deal of emphasis on the absolution pronounced by the priest after confession, there came about a striking alteration in the sacrament. In place of the sequence: confession, penance, forgiveness (i.e. being accepted) there emerged the sequence: confession, forgiveness (absolution), penance. And what is more, the penance was whittled down to a few nominal Our Fathers and Hail Marys. This has to an increasing extent given rise to the impression that forgiveness, the remission of sin, is actually brought about in the confession. That idea has been reinforced by the heady words of absolution : I absolve you from your sins in the name of the Father. . . . Yet we have always known very well that there is something wrong with that. If you stole something, you could confess as much as you like. But you could not really be absolved unless you gave back or made restitution for what had been stolen. The same thing applied in all sorts of other situations. Always the precondition for being forgiven was to put away from you the occasion for sin.

So we should not frame the question like this : if you have made it up with your wife, do you then also have to go and confess it? We ought rather to put the question this way : where in God's name do you get the strength to keep on making it up, to keep on trying? So the pronouncement of forgiveness in the sacrament in fact entails a reorientation, an opportunity to orientate yourself in respect of your past in a different way. The opportunity, that is, to identify this or that frustration and estrangement and so to come to terms with your past. If we are called to make our peace with those whom we have wronged, we are also stimulated to go further and to accept our past. Regarded in this light, the sacrament of confession and the remission of sins signifies a real experience. Grace is palpably at work. At work in the sense that in Jesus Christ we find the motivation, the disposition and the stimulus to make forgiveness 'come true' in our lives. And that forgiveness is essential if we are to grow to the full stature of Jesus Christ.

Private confession and penitential service

Private confession and penitential service are two differing but parallel forms. Each has its own emphasis, its own potentialities. The point in both cases is that there is a clarifying, in Jesus' name, of the sinful situation and a declaration of forgiveness. In the case of private confession this occurs in a personal dialogue. Here the communal element, at any rate in the form it takes at present, drops into the background. I have gone into this already. This community aspect *is* expressed, however, in the structure of the penitential service.

What is the penitential service? In Holland, they date, roughly speaking, from 1962.* They are held three or four times a year, usually just before a major feast. A group meet in the church, as a rule, on a weekday evening. This type of service is not usually associated with the celebration of the eucharist. At the beginning, the early parts of the penitential services were a joint effort between priest and congregation: hymns were sung, prayers said, scripture was read, and the group reflected and meditated together. This was followed by the hearing of private confessions for those who wished. A number of priests were usually present. Since there was a large number of people involved, the confessions had to be heard quickly, and the confessor did not talk over things with the penitent, but simply pronounced the words of absolution. When all the confessions had been heard, the service ended with an act of thanksgiving by the whole congregation. As you can see, this sort of service was a kind of cross between private confession and a penitential rite: it probably is better called a celebration of confession than a penitential service. This particular form was chosen because of the difference of opinion that existed as to whether a penitential rite which does not include private confession has any sacramental value.

It was argued that the congregation at a penitential service do not receive the sacrament if they do not go to confession and receive absolution. In any case, a service like this does provide a splendid preparation for receiving the sacrament. In March 1965 the Dutch bishops were led by these discussions to issue a statement saying that absolution may only be given in private confession and that the emergence of the penitential service must not lead to the neglect of private confession. However, private confession continued to decline, penitential services gained in popularity, and by 1967 the 1965 statement already sounded less convincing. Many felt that to deny the sacramental character of the penitential services could not halt the decline of private confession, and was really the expression of a rather defensive pastoral policy.

At the same time, people began to have second thoughts about this type of penitential service, feeling it to be a kind of com-

---

* The author describes what has happened in Holland. But similar services now occur in many parts of the world, in schools and communities as well as in parishes.

promise. They felt that the automatic character which had so often marked the practice of confession was in fact intensified in this service: the priest hearing confessions had to limit himself to pronouncing the words of absolution, without giving any guidance to the penitent, as there was no time for this. At the present moment, we find that the old practice of confession continues to decline, and that penitential services do attract a fair number of people. They display a great diversity of structure, springing partly from the different views people have of what these services can mean. Discussion as to whether the penitential service is or is not a sacrament is at the moment of secondary importance. This is partly due to the new outlook on sacramental confession and the remission of sins, about which I have already spoken.

We may regard these two, private confession and the communal penitential service, as two complementary forms of the same sacramental proceeding. The penitential service has a more communal character. Which form one opts for will depend on the situation one happens to be in. With the penitential service there is always the danger that for some people it will fail to provide any genuine reorientation, any real liberation. The forgiveness pronounced just glances off, does not make itself felt. For the situation in which a person finds himself is sometimes so complicated that liberation from it is only possible within a personal dialogue, in which that situation can be cleared up. Only then can any prospect, any glimpse of a future, filter through. Such a person is much better served by having a good talk in the confessional. This also applies to people who just need to unburden themselves, to let everything come out; to people who want to put a particular phase of their lives behind them for good; and to people who want someone to give them a firm lead and solid guidance. The exchanges that take place in the confessional these days are, generally speaking, helpful and good; just as they can be outside the confessional, if the setting is right for a really good talk. Another point is, perhaps we should substitute some other phrase for that difficult formula: 'I absolve you from your sins in the name . . .' Perhaps we just need some form of words that proclaims that, in the name of Jesus, forgiveness is possible.

As I said earlier on, it has been remarked apropos of this whole development that the emptier the confessional, the fuller the waiting-rooms of the psychiatrists. I do not see a causal connection here. What is true is that today more than ever a lot of people find themselves at their limit. Particularly as so many of the prescribed and familiar paths of the past are becoming more and more impossible. Again and again the individual is faced with decisions that have to be made. He cannot go on leaving it all to others. Yet the fact remains that an ancient practice like confession—as we have known it for generations—cannot be revived. It does not need to be. The church must always be looking out for new ways to convey the forgiveness which is possible in Jesus' name. For we human beings cannot get by without that forgiveness. Without it we grow rigid and we grow cold; which is why, especially in our day, besides the communal penitential service, the personal encounter, personal dialogue, is so necessary. A dialogue in which a perspective on the future is opened up once more, in which the future again becomes possible: a dialogue out of which forgiveness can be realized. The penitential service too must be authentic, real. It must not be a matter of choosing the way of least resistance, in the sense that you can remain comfortably vague and anonymous, can hide yourself in the group. You are not going to get anywhere that way. It would be a good thing perhaps to link up confession and penitential service with what I have been proposing. If something cannot be put right at once, then the person who committed the wrong must do so subsequently. Generally speaking, a really illuminating and heartening personal talk (a sort of confessional conversation or dialogue) will be necessary in such cases. If amends can be made on the spot but in fact are not, then in many instances a penitential service may suffice to give people the extra little push they need.

22 Follow your conscience

How do you react to laws?

We are often told 'You must follow your own conscience'. But what does this mean? How far can we go? Can we just do whatever we like, or are there limits? And who establishes the limits?

In the last chapter we were discussing the whole area of moral life and behaviour, and I would like to come back to this now more specifically. Such a lot has been happening in this area. Great changes have come about in our sense of what may be done and what may not be done. A lot of people have lost all sense of direction. They are very unhappy about the way things are going. So you often hear remarks like: 'People carry on as they like these days; there are no limits at all; nothing is too way out.' Such remarks are very understandable. For we grew up in a period when laws and rules and regulations governed everything we did in every conceivable sphere. And usually it was very hard to see why one thing should not be done or another simply had to be done. We didn't ask 'why'. It was all simply laid down, in the order of things. One simply conformed: or else! For there was an element of compulsion behind the system. If one didn't accept it, he soon learnt that. But there was no clear conviction that the laws and regulations existed for the good of the individual.

The laws were often felt to be a burden imposed from without; so one would hear people saying that 'the church' says you must go to Mass every Sunday, you mustn't eat fish on Fridays, and so on. As though the church wanted to make things as difficult for the believer as possible. The person who thinks like that fails to realize the real purpose of any law. On this point I will let *A New Catechism* speak for a moment :

> 'Many understand by "commandment" a burden imposed upon man from outside. They imagine that they would behave quite differently if there were no commandments. But this way of thinking debases the commandments to something that would be concerned with matters of no value in themselves. Honesty, reverence for life, marital fidelity, respect for others would not be valuable in themselves, but merely precepts imposed by a God who could have chosen others. Such attitudes are often the result of an education where the good is too strongly emphasized as a system of well-defined precepts; of a general atmosphere where too much stress is laid on the extrinsic "must" and too little confidence placed in the intrinsic and spontaneous sense of values in both pupils and educators. The result is that the truth that the commandments are good in themselves is lost sight of. We people forget that they are in themselves most profound and vital values, which are already anchored in the nature of man and of the world' (p. 371).

A difficult passage, which I would like to elaborate upon in rather more detail. Then there may perhaps emerge for us also the kind of love for God's law that the Jews displayed, and that is finely expressed, for example, in Psalm 119, where it says: 'Your word is a lamp to my feet and a light to my path.'

Why are *there laws, in fact?*

I would like to divide what I have to say into three parts.

1.   One thing in life, and only one, is paramount; and that is love. This is really the only commandment there is. The other person's well-being and my own. In so far as I bring happiness to another, I find it myself. That is *the basic norm: love.* All other commandments and laws must lead back to that. Yet that looks more obvious than it is. For what do you understand, what do I understand, by love? You know how different people's views about love are. You won't build a better world just by shouting 'love one another'.

2.   So we have to be always trying to get clear what love actually requires of us. This one basic norm which is love has to be worked out in a number of directions. That is how we must see the *ten commandments.* They are *norms* that show us what 'love one another' entails for us in this or that particular circumstance. Yet even the ten commandments are fairly vague. They are very general guidelines. When do I honour my father and mother, for example? Even when, contrary to what they expect or hope for, I do what I think I have to?

3.   So it is important that I should understand more clearly what love asks of me. The norms have to be worked out in their turn in a large number of *laws and provisions*, as a way of helping us in the affairs of our daily life.

These three sections must be held very closely together. Where there is no clear sense of the connection, law becomes a burden, something that has no apparent relation to one's own well-being. On the contrary, it will be seen as barring the way to happiness, as something one follows in order to keep out of trouble, for the sake of peace and quiet. Something, in fact, to be got rid of as quickly as possible. If father says to daughter: 'Be home by twelve tonight!' the girl must do her best to understand that what her father is insisting upon is good for her, that in the end her own happiness and well-being are involved. If she is quite unable to see that, if she feels unable to talking it over with her father, if she gets the idea that father is insisting on it just to be awkward or because it is what *he* once had to do, she will find it very hard to accept. Perhaps a diagram may help to make all this clearer.

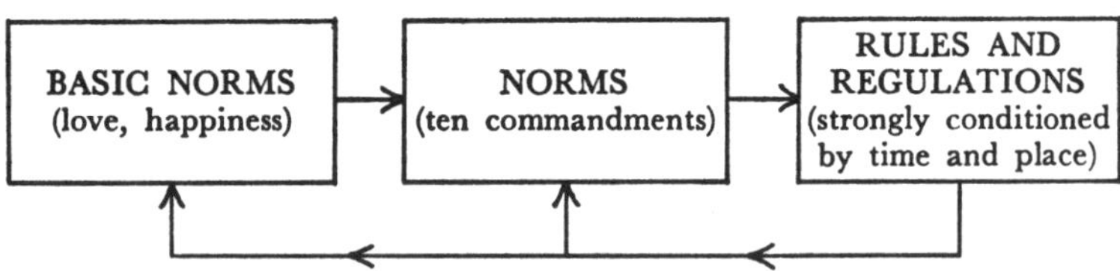

Our upbringing has been strongly rooted, so to speak, in this third section and our lives have been very largely based upon it, without any clear sense of its connection with the first section. The third section provides directives for every conceivable practical situation, which makes it very susceptible to the spirit of the age. As times change, so do the applications of the norms change too. That is what is happening now. Rules and regulations are being abandoned; and this makes some people panic. 'Were we all wrong before? Were we deliberately misled before?' Because they can't see the connection between the detailed rules and regulations and the basic norms, some people are in danger of throwing the baby out with the bathwater.

Let me give an example of what I mean. The church has removed the obligation of fasting. So many people have jumped to the conclusion that fasting, or any ascetic practice of that kind, is totally unnecessary. They fail to see that behind the fasting regulations lay the principle that it is important to have discipline in one's life. They had become so familiar with one particular form of discipline that now that it is not obligatory the whole idea of discipline threatens to disappear too.

As a kind of reaction against earlier times we are now seeing a tremendous emphasis being placed on the basic norm: love. It is the 'in word' of the hippie-movement. Love is the thing. Everything else is superfluous. That is the basis on which they mean to live, to explore living, to experiment; and on that basis they mean to try to discover or rediscover practical applications that will suit our day and age. Along with all this goes a rebelliousness aimed at existing laws and structures; so that society comes under attack, amid a general buzz of criticism. That is a good thing, of course, as regards laws and structures which are out of date; which no longer protect and serve the human person but stand in the way of his happiness. But as things stand today, a lot of people are simply against all existing laws and institutions. You might say that they, in their turn, are showing very little understanding of what laws and institutions are really in aid of. These things are not bad in themselves, whether they exist in the economic sector, in education, in the political sphere or within marriage. Practical rules are necessary. So often, what is wrong with the rules is that they make you lose sight of the norms, and of the basic norm. Then a person feels crushed under a welter of regulations and prescriptions. And that is what things were like in the immediate past.

The *advantage* of rules is that you know precisely where you stand. They make life that much easier. You know what is allowed and what isn't.

It is in the context of these alternative but divergent ways of apprehending concrete rules that we have to interpret the sort of remarks you hear, now that so many rules are going by the board. On the one hand you hear: 'That's great! you're free at last! What a relief! No more strings!' From the other side you have: 'You don't know where you are now. The bishops should speak out more clearly.'

The ten commandments

In the previous section I made a threefold distinction: between the basic norm of love, the norms (the ten commandments) and specific laws and regulations.

I would now like to say a little more about the second section: the ten commandments. Actually, they are the ten dicta, the ten 'clauses' of the covenant. Where did they come from? Did they reach us cut and dried and ready for use, so to speak? You certainly get that impression when you read in scripture how Yahweh gave these commandments to Moses on Mount Sinai; and even more so if you see how the scene is depicted in a film like 'The Ten Commandments'; and this is reflected in sayings like: 'God has inscribed the Ten Commandments upon the hearts of men.' Now what do expressions of that sort really mean? We should not ask whether man discovered the Ten Commandments for himself, or whether they were 'given' to him: this is a false antithesis. *A New Catechism* says:

> 'The story of Sinai is the succinct expression . . . of a long historical process. Once God had begun to reveal himself so effectively and so personally in the faith and history of Israel, the proper attitude to be taken towards him became clearer and clearer and was enshrined in the ten commandments'
> (p. 372).

How are we to understand this? The possible meaning of human life has only very gradually become apparent to men. They have slowly discovered the hitherto unsuspected potentiality that lies within their grasp. Only very gradually have their eyes opened to these possibilities. In Jesus, in the way he lived and the things he said, this potentiality became most profoundly apparent. He took as his starting point the basic ideal of love, in a much more definite and obvious way than the old covenant did. He 'reduced' all norms and all regulations to this ideal. As he says (Matthew 5:17): 'I have come not to abolish the law and the prophets, but to fulfil them.' So to the question 'Where do the Ten Commandments come from?' we must reply: they come from God and also from men. God works through people. When he is at work, he does not cut men out. On the contrary. He stirs them into activity. God is not in competition with man. The norms that we call the Ten Commandments are so broad, so spacious, that every culture understands them differently. Even Jesus in the Sermon on the Mount gave them a new interpretation: 'You have heard that it was said to our forefathers: You shall not kill. But I say to you: whoever is angry with his brother is liable to the judgment' (Matthew 5). The church, too, has interpreted the Ten Commandments in its own way. That is at once apparent, for instance, from the way things are put. In the biblical version of the Ten Commandments it says: 'You shall not commit adultery.' Under the influence of a climate in which *everything* to do with sex was taboo, this commandment was expanded into: 'You shall do nothing unchaste.' We, too, interpret the Ten Commandments in our own way, appropriate to our times.

Perhaps it would be of interest to take a look at how we encounter one or two of the Ten Commandments in our own day and in our own experience.

Let us take first the fifth commandment: *You shall not kill.* Put like that, it seems plain enough. And most of us would say: 'Well, that's an easy one, so far as I'm concerned.' But things are quite different if we turn it into the injunction: You shall have reverence for life. *That* is just what Jesus did in the Sermon on the Mount. You can then envisage death and life in a daily context. And then at once the difficulties begin. For what are we to do about abortion? Is it murder? Is it invariably murder? The welfare of two living beings is always directly involved here. Can you make general rules about this? And what are we to make of euthanasia (inducing death to release a person from his sufferings)? Can euthanasia result from love between husband and wife? Can they come to this decision out of love for each other? Or is that nonsense? And what should we do about the death penalty? No problem there? May we dispose of someone else's life? You can also think of life and death in a mental context. We often lose sight of the fact that people can be assassinated by public opinion, by hostile action, by distrust, by an absence of forgiveness.

We can approach the sixth commandment in this way: *You shall not do anything unchaste.* Here again the truth applies that we are not to measure the breaking of the commandment by the outward act. The same actions can be prompted by genuine love or by a kind of bestial egotism. Here again the emphasis must be put not so much on what is done, but on the attitude with which it is done. Is it done out of love or not? That has all sorts of consequences, of course, for the care and education of young peple. If, for instance, a youngster says, regarding his relationship with a girl: 'Why shouldn't I?' it doesn't make all that much sense to say: 'Because it's wrong!' You do better in such a case to ask: 'Are you fond of that girl? Are you very fond of her?' If he is not fond of her, what he is doing is immoral; and if he is fond of her, then he will have too much respect for her to allow himself to take all kinds of liberties with her. The same applies to the use of contraceptives. In themselves they are neither good nor bad (setting aside the medical aspects, of course). It all depends on the attitude with which people use them. Will they or will they not lead to a loss of mutual respect? Is it all motivated by love? Again and again this question keeps recurring. A question that reflects a new climate. A climate which must not be met, therefore, with antiquated ideas—this was one of the criticisms levelled at the encyclical on birth control (*Humanae Vitae*). This same question has given rise to a renewed discussion of divorce.

Finally, a few brief thoughts on the seventh commandment: *You shall not steal.* There are various ideas nowadays about how this commandment should be interpreted. Questions are asked like: Can I do as I like with what is my own? Is it really mine? Are not the earth's commodities really intended for everybody? After all, everyone has a right to a truly human existence. Doesn't someone who has a great deal possess things that really belong to somebody else? This idea is beginning to affect our attitude to the developing countries and our thinking about the big landed interests that still exist, for example, in South America. When we have a surplus of material things, does it really belong to us, and can we do with it whatever we please? If you answer yes to those questions, then you may regard the take-over of land as a legitimate act. Another person, starting from a different set of beliefs, may regard it as stealing. So the question arises: what is stealing; who is the thief? We are also conscious today of the perennial desire men have to 'possess everything in common': we find this already in the Acts of the Apostles. We see it embodied in certain monastic communities. We see it cropping up again and again today, in the idea of the commune.

How do you 'form your conscience'?

As I was saying before, our roots lie in a period when the accent was on laws and regulations—and often people did not see what their point was. They just obeyed them—obeyed out of fear, sometimes. Was this acting according to one's conscience? And, in fact, can there be any affinity between commandment and conscience? *A New Catechism* says that there can:

> 'Commandments and conscience interpret the same values. We should be very much mistaken if we tried to make our conscience a purely private matter, our own special secret, without any links with the community. This would estrange men from one another. It would be inhuman. It is therefore very short-sighted to affirm, as one sometimes hears, that in former times men lived by the commandments (they did what they did because they had to) while now they live by their conscience (they now do good freely). Even in former times men did not act without reference to their conscience, and even at present they do not act without reference to the commands of the community. The two go together. The emphasis may be different at different times, but that is another question. . . . A good law and a well-formed conscience are therefore a help to each other' (pp. 373–374).

You might also put it like this: people did have a conscience, but did not make use of it. 'What's happened to your conscience? Haven't you got one,' a confessor asked a penitent. 'I've got one,' he replied, 'but it's kept locked up. I never use it.' Conscience is not something or other that you have. You are your conscience. It is the way you sense good and evil, the way you work out what you have to do in a given situation.

You may wonder why there is so much talk about conscience these days. Is it because there is so much focus on the individual, and each individual is unique? Or is it because we are living in a period of transition, in which one person calls good what another calls evil? I did illustrate that with the help of the seventh commandment: You shall not steal. More possibilities occur; and confronted with them, each person has to take his pick. When someone says: 'In all conscience I can do nothing else', what does that mean? Is it an excuse for safeguarding his own decision and protecting it from further discussion? After all, a man's private conscience must be respected! When someone says: 'You must follow your own conscience over this', you may even wonder whether his advice does not reveal his impotence. Has that kind of remark ever helped anyone? Or is it just a way of leaving him high and dry? From the way people talk about conscience you would often suppose it to be so personal that it ceases to be of further concern to anyone. So you hear people say: 'Oh well, A has a flexible conscience, an elastic conscience; but B has a petty, narrow conscience. For A everything goes, for B, nothing; he gets the wind up straight away.'

This, of course, makes conscience into something quite arbitrary, on which one can place no reliance at all. What lies behind this kind of remark is the old way of looking at the question. People look to the law, but they do not perceive what it is really all about: one man happens to elevate the law, the other skips lightly over it. But they both make the same mistake. Law and rules are not the issue. The issue is the well-being of the person involved. When we talk about personal conscience, it does not mean that we make decisions of no concern to anybody else. Conscience is intended to do the exact opposite. We can only become ourselves by living for others. And conscience is meant to ensure that we become ourselves. To quote *A New Catechism*:

> 'It would be well to get rid of the bad habit of thought by which people are apt to see "person" and "society" as primarily opposed to each other. More basic and primordial than any conflict is the fact that justice can only be done to either

of them when both are taken together. The more a being is itself, the more it is together with others, the more open to give and receive, even the things of God. And vice versa, the more a being is open to others, the more truly it is itself. . . . "Self" and "together" are not ultimately opposites' (p. 373).

An individual can only have a truthworthy knowledge of good and evil, and so can only follow his conscience, if and when he is in dialogue with others: with examples who attract him, with friends and supporters, with those who think differently and those who think like himself. This 'dialogue' can even be with someone who is not present or who is no longer alive, someone who is able to inspire us by his example or through his writings. We must therefore query such remarks as: they simply don't understand my situation, and so can't understand the decisions I am making, either. If other people can in no way enter into my situation, that may very possibly be an indication that in such circumstances I should not be making decisions. To say: I cannot in all conscience justify this, ought to mean something like: this is not good for myself and for others. To say: in good conscience I must do this, implies: I must do it, because it will entail happiness for myself and for others.

Through the exercise of my conscience I am able to grow into a person, a complete person, an authentic personality. I shall become myself to the extent that I am accepted by others and in so far as I am able to accept others.

Law has occupied such a central position that we have almost come to forget that example is more powerful than any given norm, whatever it may be. 'Words alert, but deeds convert.' It is precisely in our candid intercourse and fellowship with others that we can come to see clearly what the norms and laws entail for us in a given situation. For norms and laws still have their part to play in our lives. They form a kind of communal conscience. As I said before, they are greatly conditioned by factors of place and time. They attempt to clarify what 'happiness' involves for us. Just because laws are so closely tied to place and time, because they can never provide for every situation we find ourselves in, there will always be a persistent tension between law and conscience. Law has a role to play in our decisions; but it does not make our decisions superfluous. It is inadmissable, therefore, to foist our decisions on to the law. We must choose for ourselves, however hard that may sometimes be. One person will feel the difficulty more than another. But we all know how hard it is to keep making right decisions in our lives. If you opt for one thing, you have to renounce the other. And we would much rather opt for both at the same time. So you have yourself to blame, if you choose wrong. If your choice is forced out of you by a law or by somebody above you, then you can shift the blame for failure on to other people. That gives you a much nicer feeling. A lot of people, if they could no longer lash out against laws and persons in authority, would find life hard going.

12 Beyond death

A belief called in question

Finally, I would like to try and say something to you about eternal life. I know that I have set myself a hard task. Some years ago the German theologian, Urs von Balthasar, said: 'That section of theology that deals with the last things is "closed for alterations".' Yet I suspect that you will appreciate my tackling the question: for what happens after death has been the subject of a lot of discussion lately. It is safe to say that most young people take a pretty sceptical line about the whole thing. Once again, we must ask ourselves 'Why'. Why has a belief, an article of faith, so firmly anchored in the Bible, come today to arouse so much opposition and even flat contradiction?

> 'I know nothing about it, and frankly it does not interest me all that much. After all, what conceivable bearing could a view on a life after death have on our life here and now? I don't see it. I don't believe that eternal life is a factor that can play a part in my life, any more than God is an operative factor. Therefore I can take no position on this, either to deny or to affirm it. If we go on after death in one way or another, if things gets better, well, that's fine. But if not, then surely it doesn't change my life's work in any way.'*

Sentiments like these become increasingly audible; and they are coming from people who really do want to be Christian.

The cocksure way Christians have talked about heaven in the past does carry certain dangers with it. The challenge to us to

---

* From an article in a Dutch newspaper.

115

justify 'the hope that is in us' grows more and more insistent. So it is not surprising that the Dutch bishops devoted one of their pastoral letters to this subject. In it they gave a striking testimony to their faith. I would like you to read what they had to say about life after death :

'Sisters and brothers, we . . . live eternally. The Lord died and rose again as the first among many brethren. We shall die, but after our death we shall live again with Christ. Belief in eternal life is becoming weaker among us. Many doubt, or are in a state of uncertainty about it. We understand this : we too are human beings and know uncertainty and doubt. We cannot imagine an eternal life; and that is why it is so hard to accept. Faith demands the capacity to recognize that there is more than we can hear or see, more than we can touch or handle or determine with precision by the methods of science. Unbelief stops short at the appearance presented by *this* world, it accepts only what one can envisage. . . . We cannot represent or en-visage this, but we must certainly believe it.'

The picture was too clear-cut

What is the background to this confused situation? Perhaps we should first examine in broad outline how we used to picture eternal life and what it meant to us. That picture exactly fitted the way people felt about life not so long ago. That general climate is something we have already discussed. The world was wicked, nay, a necessary evil. Outside the church there was no good, no salvation. You staked everything on the hereafter. You would be able to compensate liberally up there for what you had to do without down here. And until then you had to stick it out here below. You had to remain as unsullied as you could on the journey through this world in order to merit the hereafter. The aspect of reward and punishment played a major role in this situation. And along with that went the fear of not making it. *In that atmosphere there was a great divide between life here and life hereafter.* We were given clear and distinct notions of the hereafter. Indeed, a certain explicitness characterized that whole period. We conceived of heaven as an ideal place; and heavenly bliss went on for an unlimited length of time.

This way of representing things was tailored, as it were, to the requirements of our life-style. The concepts of time and space provided us with a good way of imagining heaven, hell and—for Catholics at least—purgatory. Then again, we were well able to conceive how the individual life could continue. We were taught that a human being came into existence by means of the parents who produced the body and of God who inserted the soul. When a person died, his soul was taken up and his body was buried; and on the general day of judgment soul and body were reunited with each other. Bound up with that was the church's horror of cremation—something the church still feels, in fact.

A great change has taken place in this way of representing and feeling about things. The whole climate in which we live has altered. We are no longer passive, unable to alter things. We ourselves are in charge. God creates through us. We have the mandate to make this world really fit to live in, for everybody. It only makes sense to talk about the glorious future that awaits us if we build that future now. We have to create the evidence for that future now. Even the disciples were supposed to witness to that future: the Kingdom of God is at hand, but at the same time they had to bring into being the signs of the Kingdom, the evidence for it, expel the powers by which men were held prisoner and heal the ailments from which men were suffering. There is no absolute gap between what is now and what is to come. We are already en route for the new heaven and the new earth promised to us. The kingdom of God is in your midst.

With this change of climate the confidently explicit way of representing the after-life has gone, too. We have become aware that we cannot form a distinct picture of the hereafter. Nobody can give an eye-witness account of it. If we do form such a picture, well, that is our own affair. Time and space are the operative factors here. Furthermore, people are inclined to give up trying to divide man into two separable components: soul and body. This twofold division certainly provided a convenient way of showing how a person was supposed to live on after death. Nowadays we prefer to regard the individual as a unity; and we are prepared to take death very seriously indeed. Jesus did that, too. The great danger for us now is that with this particular way of approaching the subject we may throw away the belief in eternal life itself. There is a tendency to do that with all our beliefs : we throw out the baby with the bathwater. 'Survival', a continued existence, is so much identified with certain concepts people used to have, that since they have been found wanting, so too, many people have given up the idea of a continued existence. That may also be the reason why so many youngsters, when asked 'Do you believe in life after death?' say no : they reject the old concepts. The bishops say : we cannot imagine it, but we must certainly believe it. That is an important statement. The strange thing is that men cannot get along without some notion of eternity; so it is intriguing to see how each period constructs its own ideas of it.

Where does belief in life after death come from?

One irresistible question is : where does belief in a life after death come from? Did it fall from the sky? Is it of our own invention? That was Karl Marx's theory : human beings have projected a better world in order to escape from this real world with all its wretchedness. His strictures are quite understandable; for because our life on earth was undervalued, belief in a life after death did not help us directly to get to grips in a radical way with the business of this one. If belief in after-life is not something that men have invented, neither is it based on any first hand account from people who have been there. For the Jews, faith in the future life is based on the activity of God which they have experienced in the past. What God has begun, that he will also bring to fulfilment. God will not abandon the work of his hands. He is a God not of the dead but of the living, the God of Abraham, Isaac and Jacob. He is true to his promises. They see an event such as the exodus from Egypt and the journey through the wilderness as the fulfilment of God's promise, however harsh and difficult that journey was. And in its turn, this fulfilment is a new promise for the future. The supreme fulfilment of God's promise takes place in Jesus Christ. The risen Lord is in his turn the great promise to us for the future. The crucial point therefore is that faith in the future depends on the fact that God has made his presence decisively felt in the past. Whoever says 'I believe in God' is really saying at the same time that he believes in God's future.

The trouble is that we have proceeded to formulate quite

distinct and separate articles of faith. 'Believing' meant that we accepted certain religious truths. As a result of that, the infallibility of the pope, the virginity of Mary, life eternal became so many separate items, lined up side by side. The one thing that really matters is that we believe. Enshrined in that is the outlook we have, our view of the future. So it is really a mistake to ask young people: do you believe in life after death? The question invites 'no' for an answer. Anyone who really believes is not going to stop short at any frontiers—not even at the frontier of death.

Every period has its own ideas about this

'We must believe it, though we can't imagine it.' Yet generation after generation has tried to conceive, to understand it. For the early Christians the main idea was of the future of *the totality*, the future of the whole of creation. Paul echoes this: 'Creation also looks with eager longing for the moment when the glory of the children of God shall be made manifest' (Romans 8:18). How we see that future depends very much on the situation in which we live. Broadly speaking, you can say: *if things are going well with people*, they tend to see the glorious future as very much an extension of life here and now.

The prophets saw the *shalom* they speak about as being continuous with what they were witnessing in their own day. When they spoke of the future, it was in order to urge people to decision and activity in the present. We too are beginning to regard the future to which we are on the way more definitely as an extension of our life now. *If things are going badly for people,* they see the future much more as a break with the present state of affairs. In the Old Testament we see that, for example, at the time of the Maccabees. The whole Jewish world at that period was in danger of being overrun by the Hellenes. The Book of Daniel was written then. It depicts in bizarre and extravagant colours the end of all things, a catastrophe of tremendous proportions. The new Kingdom will break in, the present one be destroyed.

In the years that now lie behind us—those of the second world war, especially—there was the same sort of mood. The world was evil; you could expect nothing from it. Heaven was a totally different world, therefore, which had very little connection with this one. Only in this case the accent was less on the new life of the whole of creation and much more on the continued existence of the individual.

What about me? Shall I have eternal life?

When did this belief in *personal* survival actually emerge? If the whole, the totality, has a future, if indeed God does not abandon the work of his hands, then also each and every human being is in the hand of God. The prophet Isaiah was the first to express this belief (Isaiah 26:19). It is a fact that in the time of Jesus nearly all Jews believed in a resurrection of the dead. The Sadducees did not; they believed only what was in the most ancient writings. But belief in a life after death is not something that Jesus was the first to teach or that started with his resurrection. It is true, though, that from that moment on our resurrection is linked to Jesus. This comes out strongly in the eleventh chapter of John. Martha is angry with Jesus. Her brother Lazarus is dead; and Martha finds little consolation in the thought of resurrection from the dead on the last day. She is very puzzled by it. Then Jesus says: 'I *am* the resurrection and the life. . . . Do you believe *this*?' The risen Lord means the redemption of a pledge, a pledge and promise without parallel. We have to see his resurrection against the background of God's creation. In Jesus the fulfilment of the creation is made present, existent, in the first stage of its infancy.

As regards personal survival, there are many differing notions. I shall mention a few here. For a very long period of time, Greek thought influenced the western way of thinking about things. Now, in ancient Greek culture, the contemplation of things was an ideal to be striven for. If contemplation is the ideal, then heaven will mean the contemplation of God: a blissful gazing upon God. This notion prevailed for many centuries. Now think of the nineteenth century, when the growth of industry brought with it unbearably long working hours for the majority of people. They had hardly time to draw breath. So what is the natural way for a Victorian factory hand to imagine heaven? He longs for rest, rest eternal. The man of leisure—and today we are all on the way to becoming men of leisure—is much more attracted by the images of heaven that we find in the Gospel: the banquet, the marriage feast, a social gathering. We do need to form some personal picture for ourselves, even though we know that it is bound to be only relative, and that it is dangerous to make too much of it.

In conclusion, I would like you to see how two writers, both faced with the same question, have tried, no doubt with faltering pen, to answer it. Paul answers the question: How do the dead rise? What kind of body will they have?

'Someone may ask, "How are dead people raised, and what sort of body do they have when they come back?" They are stupid questions. Whatever you sow in the ground has to die before it is given new life, and the thing that you sow is not what is going to come; you sow a bare grain, say of wheat or something like that, and then God gives it the sort of body that he has chosen: each sort of seed gets its own sort of body. Everything that is flesh is not the same flesh: there is human flesh, animals' flesh, the flesh of birds and the flesh of fish. Then there are heavenly bodies and there are earthly bodies; but the heavenly bodies have a beauty of their own and the earthly bodies a different one. The sun has its brightness, the moon a different brightness, and the stars a different brightness, and the stars differ from each other in brightness. It is the same with the resurrection of the dead: the thing that is sown is perishable but what is raised is imperishable; the thing that is sown is contemptible but what is raised is glorious; the thing that is sown is weak but what is raised is powerful; when it is sown it embodies the soul, when it is raised it embodies the spirit. If the soul has its own embodiment, so does the spirit have its own embodiment. The first man, Adam, as scripture says, became a living soul; but the last Adam has become a life-giving spirit. That is, first the one with the soul, not the spirit, and after that, the one with the spirit. The first man, being from the earth, is earthly by nature; the second man is from heaven. As this earthly man was, so are we on earth; and as the heavenly man is, so are we in heaven. And we, who have been modelled on the earthly man, will be modelled on the heavenly man.

'Or else, brothers, put it this way: flesh and blood cannot inherit the kingdom of God: and the perishable cannot inherit what lasts for ever. I will tell you something that has been secret: that we are not all going to die, but we shall all be changed. This will be instantaneous, in the twinkling of an eye, when the last trumpet sounds. It will sound, and the dead will be raised, imperishable, and we shall be changed as well, because our present perishable nature must put on imperishability and this mortal nature must put on immortality. When this perishable nature has put on imperishability, and when this mortal nature has put on immortality, then the words of scripture will come true: Death is swallowed up in victory. Death, where is your victory? Death, where is your sting? Now the sting of death is sin, and sin gets its power from the Law. So let us thank God for giving us the victory through our Lord Jesus Christ.

'Never give in then, my dear brothers, never admit defeat; keep on working at the Lord's work always, knowing that, in the Lord, you cannot be labouring in vain' (I Corinthians 15:35–58).

As Paul seems to recognize the relative nature of his reasoning, he says: keep on working at the Lord's work always, knowing that, in the Lord, you cannot be labouring in vain.

The author of *A New Catechism* also finds himself facing this question: Does nothing remain of a man? Does he just vanish, and is no more? His approach is very different from St Paul's:

'Does nothing of man really remain? Has the dead person utterly disappeared? Is the love and insight of a human life suddenly extinguished at death?—No; the warmth and light which someone has spread continue to live in others. It is marvellous how strong a person's influence can remain after death. Most creative of all is the effectiveness of a good life. And this continues in mankind even when the memory of the name and person has completely vanished. The good done by someone long ago to a child's grandmother can still be one of the factors moulding the child's life. The insights and affection of thousands long dead live on in the present day. The dead are still among us.

'But surely not in person?—But perhaps they live on in this way more personally than we often imagine. After all, what is more a man's own than the warmth of his love and the light of his wisdom?

'This is uniquely verified in the life of Jesus of Nazareth. Since he died and was buried, his spirit has never ceased to be active. On the contrary, he still stirs men's conscience and renews their lives by his love, his words and his power. He has a deeper influence on more men than any who are alive today. It seems as though his death does not matter. While our own great-great-grandfathers are often hardly even names to us, Christ remains a real person.

'It may still be said that no matter how "personal" the influence of one who is dead and gone, it is still not the man himself. Surely the self, the person, has disappeared? Let us first consider Christ once more. He is not merely recalled and admired from afar, like Rembrandt or Madame Curie. He is spoken to and loved. When we remember him in our liturgy, he is among us. We recognize that he lives, and lives in the truest sense of the word. His influence on mankind is so deep and marvellous precisely because he *himself* is present through his spirit. He is with us, to exhort, strengthen and console' (*A New Catechism*, p. 471).

So have others tried to express life after death. We cannot conceive of it. We must believe it.